DevOps Overture

What You Need to Know When Starting a DevOps Journey

Shawn D. Doyle

ReleaseTEAM Press

DevOps Overture

What You Need to Know When Starting a DevOps Journey

By Shawn D. Doyle

Copyright © 2020 Shawn D. Doyle

All rights reserved.

Printed in the United States of America.

ISBN 13: 978-0-578-62580-5 (Print)

ISBN 10: 0-578-62580-6 (Print)

ISBN 13: 978-0-578-62581-2 (EPUB)

ISBN 10: 0-578-62581-4 (EPUB)

Library of Congress Control Number: 2019920708

Editor: Kate Shoup

Production Editor: Keith Abbott

Cover Designer: Mindy Soung

Interior Designer and Layout: Shawn Morningstar

Illustrator: Mindy Soung

Indexer: Kelly Talbot Editing Services

Proofreader: Kelly Talbot Editing Services

For information on distribution, translations, or bulk sales,
please contact ReleaseTEAM Press directly.

ReleaseTEAM Press

c/o ReleaseTEAM, Inc.

1400 W 122nd Ave, Suite 202

Westminster, CO 80234

editor@releaseteampress.com

www.releaseteampress.com

Appendix C

Introduction

A few years back, I had a consulting gig with a company that wanted to transition to DevOps. One day, while I was at the company's main office, a guy approached me. I'll call him Carl. Carl asked if I'd be willing to grab dinner with him that evening to talk shop. This was a little unusual. I hadn't met Carl before, and he wasn't directly involved in the project I was working on, but I agreed.

Carl and I met at a nice restaurant. After we ordered, Carl got to the point. He explained that he'd worked as a systems administrator for decades using the same set of tools. He was worried that my work with the company would render his skill set obsolete and would put him out of a job. To save his future, Carl wanted me to tell him how he could adjust to a DevOps environment.

Over the next few hours, I told Carl what he needed to know. I explained what DevOps was and where it came from. I described the basic principles and practices of DevOps. I counseled him on how his role might change under DevOps and what he might do to prepare, and I cautioned him on some pitfalls to avoid in a DevOps effort. And I suggested some books, blogs, podcasts, and courses he might check out to get himself up to speed.

Carl wasn't the first person to ask me about DevOps, nor was he the last. Honestly, I get asked about DevOps all the time. Some people who ask me about DevOps are like Carl. Their companies have adopted DevOps and they need to adapt or be left behind. Others work for companies that don't do DevOps but want to either switch to one that does or encourage their own company to adopt DevOps practices.

I wrote this book to help these people. I believe in DevOps practices and I automate everything I can. This book is my way of automating my advice for people interested in DevOps. It's my attempt to guide those who want to gain a better understanding of DevOps, regardless of whether they work in IT or other business areas.

This book starts by recapping what came before DevOps: work models like waterfall, the Toyota Production System (TPS), total quality management (TQM), incremental and iterative development, Lean, and Agile. That's in Chapter 1, "Before DevOps."

Chapter 2, "DevOps to the Rescue," explains what DevOps is and how it works. It also introduces the three keys of DevOps: maximizing flow, obtaining fast feedback, and fostering a positive learning culture. These are a variation on something DevOps expert Gene Kim calls the Three Ways.

Chapter 3, "Maximizing Flow," Chapter 4, "Obtaining Fast Feedback," and Chapter 5, "Fostering a Positive Learning Culture," explore each of the three keys in more detail and provide concrete examples of practices and tools to achieve them. Together, these chapters provide the foundation needed to understand what DevOps is and how it works.

Chapter 6, "DevOps Roles," was written to help IT professionals in more traditional environments—people like Carl—map their experience to DevOps. The chapter lists several key DevOps roles and explains how they differ (or don't) from more traditional IT positions. Chapter 7, "Positioning Yourself for a Career in DevOps," discusses critical skills, knowledge, training, education, and personal qualities, behaviors, and attitudes needed to facilitate a leap to DevOps.

Finally, Chapter 8, "Steering Clear of Common Pitfalls," lists obstacles to switching to DevOps and practical tips to avoid them. While this information is geared more toward company leaders, it remains instructive for individuals responsible for implementing DevOps.

This book also features three appendixes. Appendix A, "DevOps Resources," lists scores of additional sources for information, including books, websites, blogs, newsletters, podcasts, online courses, webinars, organizations, conferences, and more. Appendix B, "Tools for DevOps Success," cites hundreds of tools, and Appendix C, "Glossary," defines several DevOps-related terms.

Armed with the information in this book, everyone can position themselves for success in a DevOps environment—whether they already work in one, want to move to one, or want to build one themselves.

1

Before DevOps

"If you don't have a competitive advantage, don't compete."

–Jack Welch

In This Chapter:
- The Waterfall Model
- Problems with the Waterfall Model
- Responses to the Waterfall Model

All organizations need some type of competitive advantage to survive. Often, the source of competitive advantage is quick time to market. Sometimes it's an ability to innovate or to learn and to act on that learning. Or maybe it's teamwork—like how a good pit crew provides a competitive advantage in an automobile race. Or it could be a positive organizational culture. And so on.

Oddly, few companies exploit these sources of competitive advantage. If anything, they do the opposite. They're slow to market. They don't innovate, or learn, or act on their learning. They impede teamwork. They create a toxic organizational culture. You get the idea.

Why do companies do this? Well, there are lots of reasons. But one of them is that most companies are mired in old, outdated ways of working.

This chapter explores the most prevalent old-school approach to working, called *waterfall*, and the problems inherent in this model. This chapter also covers various work models that attempted to address waterfall's problems: the Toyota Production System (TPS), total quality management (TQM), incremental and iterative development, Lean, and Agile. Aspects of these models formed the basis of DevOps, so it's good to know a little bit about them.

1

The Waterfall Model

For decades, countless organizations, including software companies, have employed a workflow model called *waterfall*. This process-intensive model breaks development activities into a series of phases that are completed one at a time and sequentially. Each one of these phases cascades into the next (hence the name).

For software development, the phases of the waterfall model are roughly as follows.

1. REQUIREMENTS: The product team documents in broad terms what the software product or feature will do.

2. DESIGN: Adhering to the requirements set forth by the product team, the design team designs the product or feature and indicates which tools and technologies to use to build it.

3. DEVELOPMENT: Using the tools and technologies specified by the design team, the development team builds the product or feature.

4. TESTING: The development team passes the product or feature to the quality assurance (QA) and information security (infosec) teams for testing. This phase often reveals bugs and security flaws that require additional design and development to correct—time permitting.

5. DEPLOYMENT: When the development team deems the product or feature ready for release, the operations team deploys it to a live environment.

6. MAINTENANCE: After the product or feature is deployed, the operations team maintains it. That can mean, for example, patching it to address bugs or security flaws or updating it to include new features.

NOTE

The phases listed here may deviate depending on the project or organization, but in general, they apply.

Problems with the Waterfall Model

Although widely used, the waterfall model presents serious problems for software development—problems that rob companies of their competitive advantage.

Here are just a few problems associated with using the waterfall model for software development, which are discussed further in the following sections.

- The development cycle takes too long.
- There's a lack of timely feedback and learning.
- Teams become siloed.
- It creates a toxic organizational culture.
- It stifles innovation.

NOTE

Did you notice how this list of problems is basically the opposite of the sources of competitive advantage described in the first paragraph of this chapter?

When Waterfall Works

Waterfall is not all bad. It offers considerable control over the development cycle and can result in a more predictable product outcome. In some scenarios, it works very well. For example, suppose you just won a ten-year government contract to build a spacecraft. You need to be absolutely certain you deliver exactly what the contract calls for, and you have zero market pressure to account for. In this case, waterfall might be the right model for you! But when a large project calls for agility in the face of market pressure, an Agile approach will likely work better. To borrow from economist Robert S. Ellinger, waterfall worked to get us to the moon, but it took Agile to build the airline industry.

Long Development Cycle

Because the waterfall model requires software teams to complete one phase of a project before advancing to the next one, the design team can't start work until the product team wraps things up; the development team can't start until the design team is done; and so on. This approach results in delays. Lots of them.

Frequent handoffs from one team to another compound these delays. Handoffs often result in work queues, which inevitably add time to the process. Short queues might be somewhat manageable, but long queues? Not so much. When a work queue becomes too long, a bottleneck forms. (A *bottleneck* is any point in the system that stems the flow.) This bottleneck slows the flow of work, adding more delays.

NOTE
Think of an automobile assembly line. If the station in charge of welding the frame falls behind, a bottleneck forms that starves every station after it of work. The same thing happens with software development.

Because of these delays, development cycles and lead times in the waterfall model tend to be very long—months or perhaps even years. These long development cycles have critical consequences:

- MISSED MARKET OPPORTUNITIES: By the time a product steps through each phase of the waterfall process and is released to market, the market may already have moved on.

- LACK OF AGILITY: Long development cycles make it impossible to react quickly to new market information.

- ADDED RISK: Organizations that operate on a long development cycle must invest hefty sums up front that they might not recoup —for example, if the bottom of the market for the product drops out two years into a four-year development cycle.

- DEATH MARCH DEPLOYMENTS: In the waterfall model, because deployments happen all at once at the tail end of a long development cycle, they tend to be complex, cumbersome, and error-prone, and last for hours or even days. Also, they often occur during off hours—nights and weekends—to minimize their impact on users. This places a significant burden on the operations teams who perform these deployments (not to mention their families).

Lack of Timely Feedback

Because the waterfall development cycle takes so long, it might be months before a designer or developer receives feedback on their product or feature from the QA and infosec teams downstream. Customer feedback takes even longer.

There are serious ramifications to this lack of timely feedback—especially when the feedback is negative. One is that designers and developers don't really learn from it. Think about it: Do you remember the thought process behind every decision you made six months ago? Neither do designers or developers. So, when they find out that some product or feature they worked on way back when doesn't operate as planned, odds are they'll have little to no idea why, or how best to fix it. (Of course, all this assumes the designer or developer still works for your company. Given how quickly people jump from job to job, this might not be the case!)

More importantly, a lack of timely feedback—specifically, customer feedback—reduces the chances that the software or feature will succeed in the marketplace. Here's why: Research indicates that between 60 and 90 percent of ideas for software products, features, or anything else are awful. Even ideas that seem amazing often deliver zero or negative value. Timely customer feedback enables designers and developers to weed out craptastic ideas early, before they waste too much time on them.

Siloed Teams

Software companies that employ a waterfall development model typically organize themselves into large, function-based teams—for example, one team each for product, design, development, QA, infosec, operations, and so on. Often, these teams are siloed. They work in near-complete isolation from each other—more like rival fiefdoms than like members of the same organization who share the same basic set of goals —not to mention ideas for efficiency, alignment, and collaboration.

Some siloed teams are figuratively isolated. They might work on the same floor or in the same building, but they don't really interact much. Other siloed teams are literally isolated. That is, they work in a different building, a different city or state, or even a different country. Teams that are isolated in this way often have an even harder time working together.

Siloed teams pose a variety of problems. Chief among these is the us-versus-them mentality that inevitably develops between them. When this happens, the members of one team view members of every other team with suspicion, hostility, and even fear, and blame them when things go wrong. Obviously, this hampers communication and cooperation!

To make matters worse, siloed teams are often at cross-purposes with each other. Take the development and operations teams, for example. The development team's purpose is to build and release new products and features as quickly as possible. The operations team's purpose is to ensure products and features are stable, reliable, and secure. These purposes are diametrically opposed. It's no wonder these two teams regularly grumble about each other.

Finally, projects involving siloed teams often take longer. One reason for this is the aforementioned number of handoffs required. Another is that so-called *upstream* teams (product, design, and development) rarely know what later-stage *downstream* teams (QA, infosec, and operations) need in order to function properly. For example, development teams rarely identify, let alone implement, ways to expedite the work of operations teams.

Organizational Structure

Organizations that employ the waterfall work model tend to be more traditional in nature. Not surprisingly, they also typically employ a more traditional hierarchical organizational structure.

A hierarchical organizational structure looks like a pyramid. At the top is the organization's CEO. Below that person is a small layer of managers. Below them is a larger layer of managers, and then an even larger layer of managers, and so on.

Hierarchical organizations stand in contrast to organizations with a flat organizational structure. Flat organizations have fewer layers between top leaders and rank-and-file workers and generally allow for greater autonomy across the board.

Hierarchical organizations do offer certain advantages. For example, there's a clear chain of command, employees know their roles and where they fit in the hierarchy, and there's a clear path for promotion.

But there are disadvantages, too, many of which relate to the sources of competitive advantage discussed earlier:

- THEY'RE BUREAUCRATIC: This results in delays, which lengthens the development cycle.

- THEY LIMIT LEARNING AND INNOVATION: Information and instructions flow from the top down. Lower-level employees have limited freedom to experiment, and they rarely share new knowledge upward beyond their immediate supervisor.

- THEY IMPEDE COLLABORATION: Teams in hierarchical organizations often become territorial. They refuse to share information or ask for help, which hampers collaboration.

- THEY'RE BAD FOR MORALE: Hierarchical structures promote inequality, which creates a toxic organizational culture.

Potentially Toxic Organizational Culture

The heavily process-oriented nature of the waterfall model, the indifferent or even adversarial relationships between siloed teams, and the top-down hierarchical structure employed by most waterfall organizations tend to result in a toxic organizational culture, in which employees feel frustrated, unhappy, and powerless.

This type of culture is bad for employees. *Really* bad—particularly when it makes employees feel powerless. Indeed, psychologists say that inflicting systems that rob people of their sense of power is one of the worst things you can do to them. These types of systems deny people the ability to control their own destiny and often discourage them from doing the right thing for fear of failure or punishment. They also tend to trigger a condition called *burnout*, which describes a stress-induced physical or mental breakdown.

A toxic organizational culture doesn't just threaten employee health. It also threatens the organization's health. Employees who feel unhappy, frustrated, or powerless almost always disengage. Unlike engaged workers, who are passionate about their job, feel connected to their company, and are therefore energetic and innovative, disengaged workers are checked out. They may show up, but they do as little as possible and leave as soon as they can—and that's a best-case scenario.

In a worst-case scenario, a disengaged employee might undermine or even sabotage the efforts of their more engaged co-workers.

NOTE

Experts estimate that disengaged employees cost companies between $450 and $550 *billion* per year.

Stifling of Innovation

In addition to instilling in people a feeling of powerlessness, heavily process-oriented systems also hamper creativity. Because these systems suffocate natural innovators—people who like to tinker and experiment, or who are inclined to take risks—they stifle innovation.

The delays baked into the waterfall model's long development also stifle innovation—or, more precisely, the constant firefighting required to stay on schedule in the face of those delays stifles it. *Firefighting* involves taking shortcuts or putting off planned or preventive work to deal with emergencies (also called *unplanned work*). Incessantly putting out fires—reacting to one emergency after another—consumes the time and mental bandwidth necessary for innovation.

NOTE

Innovation is more than just inventing new products or features to storm the marketplace. It's also developing new, more efficient ways of working—which can then free up yet more time for innovating. Think of Henry Ford. He revolutionized the automobile industry not with his cars, but with the assembly line.

Responses to the Waterfall Model

Over the years, companies have developed several work systems to address the problems inherent in the waterfall model. These include:

- The Toyota Production System (TPS)
- Total quality management (TQM)
- Incremental and iterative development

- Lean
- Agile

The Toyota Production System (TPS)

In 1948, the Toyota Motor Corporation implemented a new manufacturing system in its automobile production plants. This system, which evolved over the next several decades, was called the *Toyota Production System* (*TPS*). TPS optimized the waterfall method to such a degree that by the 1980s, Toyota, along with other companies that adopted TPS (most hailing from Japan), had effectively cornered the worldwide automobile market.

TPS, which is often called *just-in-time* (*JIT*) *production*, has three aims:

- To make only what is needed
- To make it only when it is needed
- To make only as much of it as needed

The result is a much quicker, and much cheaper, production system.

TPS also focuses on eliminating overburden (*muri*), inconsistency (*mura*), and waste (*muda*) from the production process. Of these, waste is of particular concern. TPS identifies several types of waste:

- Transportation of products, people, or tools
- Excessive inventory
- Excessive motion by machines or people
- Wait time
- Overproduction (making too many products, making products before they are needed, or making products that aren't needed at all)
- Overprocessing (using processes with unnecessary steps or using tools that are more precise than necessary)
- Defects

Eliminating waste isn't easy. Often, eliminating waste at one point of the cycle causes it to rear its ugly head down the line—which is why one DevOps expert likens it to playing Whac-A-Mole. However, eliminating waste can help speed up processes and improve profitability.

Two underlying principles guide TPS:

- Continuous improvement (*kaizen* or *kata*)
- Respect for people

Continuous improvement describes an ongoing cycle of improving processes, services, and products. These might be sweeping improvements or incremental ones. Practices associated with continuous improvement include:

- Taking a long view
- Challenging yourself
- Using creative thinking
- Continuously striving to improve business processes
- Innovating and evolving
- Uncovering issues
- Solving root problems to drive organizational learning

Continuous improvement also calls for workers to elevate preventive work in order to improve daily work—in other words, to pay down technical debt (a long-term price for short-term decisions) or avoid it altogether. (Chapter 3, "Maximizing Flow," discusses technical debt in more detail.)

To convey respect for people, TPS practitioners make every effort to understand others and the challenges they face, and to build mutual trust. They also:

- Take responsibility
- Emphasize teamwork
- Help each other
- Stimulate personal and professional growth
- Share opportunities for training and development
- Put people before technology and processes

The result is a positive, humane organizational culture.

Total Quality Management (TQM)

Most companies that develop effective work systems keep the inner workings of those systems to themselves—particularly if they offer a competitive advantage. But Toyota willingly shared TPS, first with its own suppliers and later with other companies, mostly from Japan.

By the early 1980s, products made by Japanese companies that had adopted TPS began to surpass those made by their North American and Western European counterparts in terms of both quality and cost-efficiency. This prompted these Western companies to rethink their own production practices. The result was a new approach: *total quality management (TQM)*.

TQM was like TPS in that it optimized the waterfall approach to improve quality. Unlike TPS, however, TQM didn't emphasize the human side of things. Eventually, TQM fell out of favor.

Incremental and Iterative Development

Both TPS and TQM employed a waterfall workflow, in which each phase had to be 100-percent complete before work could flow to the next phase. During the late 1980s, software developers devised a variation on this approach called *incremental development*.

With incremental development, work still cascaded from one phase to the next, but work was broken down into smaller tasks or batch sizes. As soon as some small piece was complete—or even *mostly* complete—work could begin on the next phase.

Incremental development offered several benefits:

- Reduced cycle times
- Faster iterations
- Decreased risk
- Increased return on investment over time
- Reduced overhead
- Improved prioritization
- Increased flexibility

Some organizations combined incremental development with another approach called *iterative development*. Like incremental development, iterative development broke large projects into smaller pieces. But iterative development also bent the linear waterfall system into a circle. Code was designed, developed, and tested in iterative cycles until it was deemed ready for deployment. This allowed for greater flexibility in the face of changing requirements.

Lean

Another variation on TPS emerged in the 1980s: *Lean*. Like TPS, Lean was a humane system. It valued every individual. And like TPS, Lean's primary goal was to eliminate waste. But in addition to eliminating the varieties of waste that Toyota identified (transportation, inventory, movement, and so on), Lean sought to abolish *any* process or product that did not add value for the customer.

Lean also worked to smooth and optimize workflow. It achieved this in part by identifying bottlenecks in the system and making improvements to eliminate them. Another way it achieved this was by taking an incremental approach and working in small batches.

NOTE

Lean makes system improvements only at the bottleneck. Improving the system before the bottleneck results in a bigger jam at the bottleneck. And making improvements after the bottleneck leaves downstream employees idle.

Lean took a scientific approach. Even today, too many organizations decide what products or features to produce and how to produce them based on the whims of some senior executive rather than on research or evidence. Taking a scientific approach helped Lean organizations make more informed, and therefore more profitable, decisions.

Agile

A new approach to software development called *Agile* emerged during the 1990s. Agile combined aspects of TPS, TQM, incremental and iterative development, and Lean. It also took a lightweight approach to development, meaning it did not burden itself with excessive planning, regulation, or management.

In 2001, a group of top Agile practitioners codified its values in a document called *Manifesto for Agile Software Development*. These values were as follows:

- Individuals and interactions over processes and tools
- Working software over comprehensive documentation
- Customer collaboration over contract negotiation
- Responding to change over following a plan

The *Manifesto for Agile Software Development* also set forth several guiding principles:

- Please customers by continually delivering useful software.
- Embrace changing requirements during the development process.
- Deliver working software as frequently as you can.
- Work with other stakeholders on a daily basis.
- Give motivated employees the tools and environment they need to perform, and trust them to get things done.
- Convey important information in face-to-face conversations.
- Make working software the best measure of progress.
- Work at a constant and sustainable pace.
- Strive for technical excellence to enhance agility.
- Keep things simple and avoid unnecessary work.
- Allow teams to organize organically.
- Regularly reflect on how to become more effective, and adjust accordingly.

These values and principles helped establish Agile as the most efficient and effective software delivery model of its day. However, there were more evolutions to come—including DevOps.

Conclusion

Companies have employed the waterfall model for decades. However, this model poses several problems, including a long development cycle, lack of timely feedback, siloed teams, toxic cultural tendencies, and the stifling of innovation. All these problems make it harder for companies to enjoy a competitive advantage.

Over the years, companies have modified and optimized the waterfall model to address these and other problems. Examples of waterfall variants include TPS, TQM, incremental and iterative development, Lean, and Agile. The next chapter discusses how DevOps takes these variations even further.

2

DevOps to the Rescue

"Imagine a world where product owners, Development, QA, IT Operations, and Infosec work together."

–Gene Kim, Jez Humble,
Patrick Debois, and John Willis

In This Chapter:

- The Emergence of DevOps
- DevOps Defined
- How DevOps Works
- A Common DevOps Workflow
- Who Uses DevOps

The waterfall method of software delivery was a little like the method used to build cars before the advent of the assembly line, with craftsmen building a single car by hand before moving on to build the next one. In other words, not optimal.

As discussed in Chapter 1, "Before DevOps," many work systems evolved over several decades to address the problems inherent in the waterfall model, including:

- TPS
- TQM
- Incremental and iterative development
- Lean
- Agile

Each of these systems of work represents a variation on waterfall.

DevOps takes these variations even further and offers more significant gains—the way the fully automated assembly line offered gains for automobile manufacturers. This chapter explains how DevOps emerged, what it is, and how it works. It also steps you through a common DevOps workflow and discusses who uses DevOps.

The Emergence of DevOps

During the late 1990s, software development teams began using Agile in greater and greater numbers. There was just one problem: These development teams became so efficient at developing software it strained the operations teams downstream.

To relieve this strain, some organizations merged their development and operations groups into a series of small cross-functional teams. Then, they pressed everyone on each team—developers *and* ops specialists—to adopt Agile practices. Thus, DevOps was born.

Eventually, DevOps teams evolved to include members of more downstream groups, like QA and infosec. Some DevOps teams even include members of upstream groups, like product and design. These small cross-functional teams are a hallmark of DevOps.

NOTE

DevOps does not replace Agile; it encompasses it.

The Birth of DevOps

Most digital historians date DevOps' birth to 2009, when two Flickr engineers, John Allspaw and Paul Hammond, delivered a groundbreaking presentation at the O'Reilly Velocity Conference in San Jose. The presentation, called "10+ Deploys per Day: Dev and Ops Cooperation at Flickr," revealed how dev and ops could work together to—you guessed it—perform ten or more code deployments per day.

For organizations that performed deployments every few months at most, the premise of this presentation was borderline insane. Nonetheless, the presentation created a roadmap for merging dev and ops to improve the software-deployment process.

DevOps Defined

DevOps evolved from movements like those mentioned in Chapter 1. But what *is* DevOps, exactly?

There is no single, universally accepted definition of DevOps. For example, Amazon defines DevOps as:

> the combination of cultural philosophies, practices, and tools that increases an organization's ability to deliver applications and services at high velocity: evolving and improving products at a faster pace than organizations using traditional software development and infrastructure management processes.

Emily Freeman, author of *DevOps For Dummies*, calls it:

> an engineering culture of collaboration, ownership, and learning with the purpose of accelerating the software development life cycle from ideation to production.

And Jason Hand at *Wired* offers yet another definition:

> a culture of collaboration and sharing aimed at bringing the software development and operations teams together to help eliminate constraints and decrease time-to-market.

Me? I see DevOps as a set of technical and cultural practices that shorten the path from concept to completed project, but I believe the precise practices used, and the path itself, will differ from organization to organization.

NOTE

Most companies that use DevOps make software for use by consumers on the web, but many more types of software projects can benefit from DevOps.

How DevOps Works

Just as there is no single, universal definition of DevOps, there is no single, universal way to "do DevOps." Instead, DevOps expert Gene

Kim suggests a three-pronged approach. Kim calls this approach the *Three Ways*:

- THE FIRST WAY: Systems thinking
- THE SECOND WAY: Amplify feedback loops
- THE THIRD WAY: Culture of continual experimentation and learning

Kim's Three Ways do a great job explaining how DevOps works. In essence, they boil down to:

- Maximizing flow
- Obtaining fast feedback
- Fostering a positive learning culture

The following sections—and the next three chapters—discuss maximizing flow, obtaining fast feedback, and fostering a positive learning culture in more detail.

NOTE

Each of the Three Ways stands alone, but they also work together. That is, fostering a positive learning culture stimulates communication for fast feedback; obtaining fast feedback maximizes flow; and maximizing flow brings successes that help foster a positive learning culture.

Maximizing Flow

If your goal is to accelerate the software development life cycle, then maximizing flow is a no-brainer. This involves a few key practices:

- Assembling small, cross-functional teams
- Evaluating and optimizing the value stream
- Applying continuous delivery
- Practicing continuous improvement

The Five Ideals

In addition to the Three Ways, Gene Kim identifies what he calls the *Five Ideals* of DevOps. Many of these ideals are attained by realizing the Three Ways. Attaining the Five Ideals helps companies drive DevOps success.

The Five Ideals are:

- LOCALITY AND SIMPLICITY: Attaining this ideal means realizing the First Way: maximizing flow. The First Way calls for empowering small cross-functional teams to establish a simple architecture and workflow to quickly and independently develop, test, and deploy code that satisfies customer needs.

- FOCUS, FLOW, AND JOY: Achieving this ideal means applying energy to solving real business problems rather than handling niggling issues you'd rather not deal with or putting out fires. It also means cultivating a positive learning culture—in other words, realizing the Third Way.

- IMPROVEMENT OF DAILY WORK: Achieving this ideal requires the realization of the Second Way: amplifying feedback loops or obtaining fast feedback. Getting actionable feedback from as many sources as possible enables you to validate (or invalidate) assumptions, solve problems, and innovate. Achieving this ideal also means paying down something called *technical debt*, which is described in Chapter 3, "Maximizing Flow."

- PSYCHOLOGICAL SAFETY: Attaining this ideal means ensuring workers don't feel insecure or embarrassed. And this, in turn, involves realizing the Third Way.

- CUSTOMER FOCUS: Achieving this ideal means basing decisions on what the customer values. This means obtaining fast customer feedback, as required by the Second Way.

Implementing all (or even just some) of these practices to maximize flow offers several benefits.

- IMPROVED COLLABORATION AND TEAMWORK: Assembling cross-functional teams results in greater cooperation among functional groups.

- INCREASED SPEED: Improving the value stream and applying continuous delivery reduces both lead times and cycle times.

- FASTER TIME TO MARKET: Reduced lead times and cycle times equate to a faster time to market, which enables organizations to stake their claim in the marketplace before anyone else.

- INCREASED AGILITY: Reduced lead times and cycle times enables organizations to respond to the needs and wishes of their customers that much faster.

- EASIER DEPLOYMENTS: Applying continuous delivery results in faster, more frequent, and, therefore, less painful deployments.

- GREATER EFFICIENCY: Evaluating the value stream and practicing continuous improvement can reveal and remedy inefficiencies.

For more information on maximizing flow, see Chapter 3.

Obtaining Fast Feedback

Maximizing flow to accelerate the product development cycle is great. But if that product is poorly designed or constructed—or worse, it's the wrong product altogether—it's ultimately useless. That's where fast feedback comes in.

Obtaining fast feedback—from a variety of sources and at every stage of the development process—promotes quick learning, improves quality, and fosters innovation. According to the authors of *The DevOps Handbook*, it also helps ensure you "don't spend years building features [your] customers don't want, deploying code that doesn't work, or fixing something that isn't actually the cause of [your] problem."

NOTE

Obtaining fast feedback involves instituting mechanisms to amplify feedback and building short feedback loops into your system.

There are many forms of feedback. For best results, you'll want to collect all of them as often as you can. Here are a few examples of forms of feedback:

- Automated testing
- Telemetry
- Peers and downstream groups
- Customers

Obtaining fast feedback offers numerous advantages:

- INCREASED LEARNING: Feedback is information, information is knowledge, and knowledge is a competitive advantage.

- FASTER FAILURES AND FIXES: Some level of failure is inevitable. Fast feedback helps ensure that when failures *do* occur, they occur early in the development cycle when they're still small, easy, and less expensive to fix.

- LOWER FAILURE RATES: Fast fixes decrease failure rates—especially for the catastrophic failures that often occur late in the development cycle.

- IMPROVED QUALITY AND SECURITY: Obtaining fast feedback from QA and infosec groups ensures that quality and security are baked in.

- EASIER DEPLOYMENTS: Fast feedback from ops helps design and development groups work with deployment in mind.

- INCREASED AGILITY: Fast customer feedback helps companies sniff out changes in the marketplace before anyone else does and respond accordingly.

- HIGHER LEVELS OF CUSTOMER SATISFACTION: Giving customers products and features that they actually want makes them happier.

For more information, see Chapter 4, "Obtaining Fast Feedback."

Fostering a Positive Learning Culture

As discussed in Chapter 1, a toxic organizational culture can cause employees to feel frustrated, unhappy, and powerless. But that's not all. Toxic organizational cultures also prevent the development of trust, which inhibits innovation and learning.

Here's an example: Suppose you have a great idea to improve a critical system in your organization. You're not 100 percent sure it will work, but if it does, it will reap real benefits for the company. You bring the idea to your supervisor, who reluctantly agrees to implement it. But instead of delivering the benefits you anticipated, your idea creates a problem for a downstream group.

In an organization with a toxic organizational culture, you'd be forced to abandon the idea immediately. Worse, you'd probably be blamed and maybe even reprimanded for the mistake. So, you'd almost certainly keep your next great idea to yourself.

In contrast, in a company with a positive learning culture, you'd be encouraged to find out why the idea failed. And you'd *never* be blamed or shamed. In fact, you'd likely be encouraged to keep experimenting with the idea until you got it right or to dream up something even better—maybe even something that disrupts your whole industry and positions your company to capitalize on the disruption.

Organizations can foster a positive learning organizational culture by:

- Offering opportunities for learning
- Encouraging experimentation
- Accepting and learning from failure
- Practicing zero blame
- Building trust
- Preventing burnout
- Motivating and rewarding employees the right way
- Continuously striving to improve

In addition to boosting innovation and learning, fostering a positive learning culture promotes:

- IMPROVED COLLABORATION AND TEAMWORK: Teams no longer adopt an us-versus-them viewpoint. Instead, says Agile expert Stephen Nelson-Smith, "an 'all hands on deck' mentality emerges."
- LESS TURNOVER: People who work in positive learning cultures are more likely to be happy in their jobs and less likely to defect to competitors.

- EASIER RECRUITMENT OF TOP TALENT: Top talent can work anywhere. A positive learning culture increases the odds they'll come work for *you*.

For more information, see Chapter 5, "Fostering a Positive Learning Culture."

The Critical Metric: The Bottom Line

Nearly all the benefits associated with the Three Ways move the needle on the most critical metric of all: profitability. Improved collaboration and teamwork, increased speed, faster time to market, increased agility, easier deployments, greater efficiency, increased learning, faster fixes, lower failure rates, earlier failures, higher customer satisfaction, less turnover, and easier recruitment —all these things boost the bottom line.

A Common DevOps Workflow

The DevOps workflow isn't so different from the waterfall workflow. Broadly speaking, work passes through the following phases:

1. Requirements
2. Design
3. Development
4. Testing
5. Deployment
6. Maintenance

But with DevOps, the work passes through each of these phases in much smaller batches, much more quickly, and with much shorter feedback loops.

NOTE

Although the DevOps process can be described in waterfall terms, DevOps practitioners generally think of it as a pipeline.

DevOps also uses special tools to expedite the flow of work from phase to phase. Table 2.1 lists several types of tools used in the implementation of DevOps. Chapter 3, "Maximizing Flow," and Appendix B, "Tools for DevOps Success," discuss tools in more detail.

TABLE 2.I   Types of Tools for DevOps

Frameworks and Libraries	Collaboration	Project Management	Requirements Management
Source code management (SCM) and version control	SCM clients	Database automation	Asset management
Testing	Code review	Build management and automation	Continuous integration (CI)
Release orchestration	Continuous delivery (CD) and continuous deployment (CD)	Configuration management	Infrastructure as code
Virtual machines (VMs) and containers	Change management	Incident management	Issue tracking
Analytics	Security	IT service management (ITSM)	Tool suites and centralized tool management

Who Uses DevOps

DevOps is a model for accelerating the software development life cycle. So, it makes sense that it is used predominantly by tech companies. Here are just a few tech organizations that have successfully adopted DevOps:

- Amazon
- Etsy
- Facebook
- Flickr
- Google
- Microsoft
- Netflix

Tech companies aren't the only organizations to shift to a DevOps model, however. Top companies in countless other industries have organized their IT functions around DevOps. (See Table 2.2.) Even some U.S. government agencies, like NASA, the Army, the Air Force, the Federal Aviation Administration, and the Department of Justice, use DevOps.

TABLE 2.2   Top DevOps Companies by Industry

Industry	Companies*
Automotive	Ford and Toyota
Consumer	Best Buy, Ericsson, General Electric, LEGO, Nordstrom, Payless ShoeSource, Samsung, Staples, Target, Tiffany & Co., and Verizon
Defense	Lockheed Martin, Northrop Grumman, Raytheon, and Honeywell
Financial Services	Bank of America, BMO, Capital One, Citibank, and Freddie Mac
Travel	American Airlines, Hertz, and Marriott

*Full disclosure: Several companies on this list are ReleaseTEAM clients.

Basically, if an organization has an IT function, odds are it can use DevOps. This is because most IT functions operate a lot like a software company. Very few organizations use every piece of software they buy straight out of the box. The IT function almost always customizes it in some way. This is particularly true with industry-specific software— say, a program that tracks hotel reservations or a point-of-sale system for a large retailer. Odds are someone, somewhere in your organization, is writing code for you!

The Changing Role of IT

Businesses of all types used to see their IT function as merely "a utility that improves internal operations," say *Lean Enterprise: How High Performance Organizations Innovate at Scale* authors Jez Humble, Joanne Molesky, and Barry O'Reilly. That's starting to change. Now, more businesses see IT as a source of competitive advantage. Indeed, say Humble, Molesky, and O'Reilly, analysis shows "that firms with high-performing IT organizations were *twice as likely* to exceed their profitability, market share, and productivity goals."

Conclusion

DevOps solves many of the problems associated with more traditional work models—things like long development cycles, lack of timely feedback, siloed teams, a toxic organizational culture, and stifled innovation.

DevOps also offers many other benefits, including easier deployments, increased agility, higher customer satisfaction, improved security, and more.

DevOps achieves all this by:

- Maximizing flow
- Obtaining fast feedback
- Fostering a positive learning culture

The next three chapters discuss each of these in more detail.

3
CHAPTER Maximizing Flow

"Nothing is particularly hard if you divide it into small jobs."

–Henry Ford

In This Chapter:
- Assembling Small Cross-Functional Teams
- Evaluating and Optimizing the Value Stream
- Applying Continuous Delivery
- Practicing Continuous Improvement

As noted in Chapter 2, "DevOps to the Rescue," DevOps calls for a three-pronged approach. The first of these is maximizing flow.

Maximizing flow brings several benefits. These include:
- Improved collaboration and teamwork
- Increased speed
- Faster time to market
- Increased agility
- Easier deployments
- Greater efficiency

NOTE

Maximizing flow—or more specifically, systems thinking—also helps attain Gene Kim's First Ideal: locality and simplicity.

Improving productivity by maximizing flow is hardly new. Indeed, maximizing flow was the driving idea behind the assembly line popularized by Henry Ford during the 1910s. DevOps uses different methods to maximize flow, however. This chapter discusses some of these methods in detail.

Assembling Small Cross-Functional Teams

Recall from Chapter 2 that DevOps emerged when companies began combining their dev and ops groups and organizing them into small cross-functional teams. Later, these teams evolved to include members of other downstream groups like QA and infosec (and, in some cases, upstream groups like product and design).

NOTE

Assigning members of downstream groups into upstream teams effectively moves the tasks associated with those groups earlier, or leftward, in the development cycle. This is part of a practice called *shifting left*.

Moving members of downstream groups upstream gives them a chance to weigh in on the product or feature during development rather than waiting until after that process is complete. This means they can identify quality and security problems early on, when fixing them is still quick, easy, and cheap.

Creating these cross-functional teams also enables everyone to ensure that the product or feature is engineered with their concerns in mind. In other words, it guarantees that quality, privacy, security, maintainability, and other crucial elements are built-in. All this maximizes flow.

Finally, cross-functional teams:

- Dismantle silos that slow the software development cycle
- Defuse the us-versus-them dynamic
- Align the goals and incentives of each functional group
- Expedite communication and collaboration
- Smooth the development process

- Minimize handoffs
- Prevent bottlenecks
- Prevent security issues after the product or feature is released

Notice that teams in DevOps aren't just cross-functional. They're also small—no more than ten people, and preferably fewer than that. Each team should have only the minimum set of expertise needed to solve any one problem. Adding even one more person beyond that just makes everything harder.

NOTE

According to Amazon, two pizzas should be enough to feed an entire team. If a team needs three pizzas, the team is too big.

Small teams offer several advantages that also help maximize flow:

- They're fast.
- They're agile.
- They help prevent scope creep. (*Scope creep* describes when goals of a project expand as the project is in progress. Scope creep often causes projects to take longer than they should.)
- They allow for quick learning.
- They're easier to manage.
- They expedite communication and collaboration.
- They create less conflict.

NOTE

Small cross-functional teams are a hallmark of DevOps. Expert John Allspaw explains that "Success in modern technical endeavors absolutely requires multiple perspectives and expertise to collaborate."

Companies should allow each small cross-functional team as much autonomy as possible. Of course, the powers that be will dictate *what* each team will produce. However, each team should decide *how* it will produce it—who will do what, by what method, and with what tools.

No one knows better than the team itself how best to work effectively! This maximizes flow *and* improves morale.

Not all organizations are structured to handle small cross-functional teams. That's OK. They can still implement DevOps. One way they can do this is by peeling away a few members of their downstream teams and embedding them in upstream groups. Another way is by promoting a high level of trust among the various functional groups. (Chapter 5, "Fostering a Positive Learning Culture," talks more about trust.) As Mike Rother says in his book *Toyota Kata*: "What is decisive is not the form of the organization, but how people act and react."

TIP

There's one downside to small cross-functional teams: Engineers in the same discipline lose a sense of camaraderie because they're no longer on the same team. To mitigate this, consider organizing events to allow engineers to mingle with others in the same role.

There's No Such Thing as a "DevOps Team"

Some companies form a brand-new "DevOps team" that works independently of all others and then consider their DevOps effort complete. This doesn't fly. All it does is create yet another silo that needs breaking down.

On a related note, there's no such thing as a "DevOps engineer," either, although you'll hear plenty of people use the term. Usually, this just refers to anyone who performs some kind of engineering role in a DevOps environment.

Structuring Teams for DevOps

DevOps works best when functional groups are reorganized into teams that are small and cross-functional. But how should you structure these teams?

One common structure is a *T formation*. Teams structured in a T formation possess deep knowledge in one functional area (represented by the vertical bar of the T) and more limited proficiency in other relevant areas (signified by the horizontal bar). For example, one team's deep knowledge might be in development with proficiency in security or cloud operations, another team's deep knowledge could be in operations with proficiency in development and QA, and so on. (See Figure 3.1.)

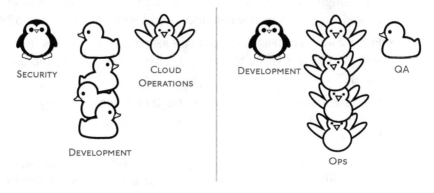

SECURITY   CLOUD OPERATIONS   DEVELOPMENT   QA

DEVELOPMENT

OPS

FIGURE 3.1 Each bird on each of these "teams" represents a different skill set.

Structuring teams in a T formation facilitates collaboration and the sharing of expertise within teams. It also facilitates it across them. For example, a member of one team who has only limited proficiency in a functional area can easily ask for guidance from a member of another team whose knowledge is deeper.

The *Π (pi) formation* is another possible structure. As you might guess, teams with this formation have deep knowledge in two functional areas or are stocked with people who are experts in two fields. A Π formation offers even greater flexibility than a T formation and is especially prevalent in smaller companies where resources are scarce.

NOTE

Your organization might be small enough to consider your entire engineering function to be one small cross-functional team. This is often the case with startups.

Ensuring Successful Teams in DevOps

A good team is like an organism or an ecosystem. It works in perfect harmony to survive and thrive. Regardless of whether companies choose a T formation, a Π formation, or some other structure, there are steps they should take to promote successful teams.

- FOSTER A SENSE OF SHARED PURPOSE: This means conveying a vision that is, in the words of the authors of Lean Enterprise, "challenging enough for the group to have something to aspire to, but clear enough so that everyone can understand what they need to do."

- ENCOURAGE TEAM MEMBERS TO SHARE RESPONSIBILITY: Teams are a little bit like the Three Musketeers: They're "all for one and one for all."

- LET TEAMS SELF-SELECT: Allowing engineers who already like, admire, and respect each other to team up is a great way to build a positive team culture.

- EMPOWER TEAMS TO WORK AUTONOMOUSLY: Yes, upper management will dictate what teams build, but it should not weigh in on how they build it. Giving teams the autonomy to use the tools and techniques they prefer not only improves their efficiency, it provides them with a powerful sense of ownership.

- MEASURE TEAM SATISFACTION: Companies should regularly survey team members to gauge how happy, motivated, and satisfied they feel.

- SUPPORT DIVERSITY: According to the authors of *Accelerate*, "Research shows that teams with more diversity with regard to gender or underrepresented minorities are smarter, achieve better team performance, and achieve better business outcomes."

Evaluating and Optimizing the Value Stream

A *value stream* describes in detail the steps that occur during a product or feature's design, development, and distribution. This sequence spans from the instant the idea is conceived to the moment the product or feature is delivered to the customer. The steps in this sequence might number in the hundreds or thousands and involve dozens of people or more.

Recruiting for DevOps

DevOps calls for more than just technical skills, so companies that want to switch to DevOps might need to adapt their recruiting tactics.

Google suggests hiring based on three key qualities:

- LEARNING ABILITY: This means finding candidates who have a growth mindset and an ability to pick up and process new information quickly. (You'll learn what a growth mindset is in Chapter 5.)

- LEADERSHIP SKILLS: This doesn't mean companies should only hire people with formal leadership training. Rather, it means identifying people who might be natural leaders but who have never assumed a conventional leadership role.

- MINDSET: Companies should seek out people who are enthusiastic, work well with others, have strong communication skills, are curious, are adaptable, and can handle failure.

To maximize flow, the value stream for a product or feature should contain only those steps that are absolutely required—nothing more, nothing less. Those steps should be performed as efficiently as possible. Too often, though, the value stream becomes bloated with waste in the form of unnecessary or inefficient steps. This might be due to any (or all) of the following:

- ENTROPY: The laws of physics dictate that all processes naturally devolve into chaos over time, including the ones in your value stream.

- LACK OF AWARENESS: Downstream groups often repeat steps completed by upstream groups simply because they are unaware of what steps have already been done.

- WORKAROUNDS: When problems arise in the value stream, time constraints often result in so-called solutions like inefficient workarounds.

- OVERKILL: Sometimes, instead of workarounds, companies try to solve problems in the value stream by introducing overly burdensome—and perhaps unnecessary—inspection and approval processes.
- TRADITION: The mentality that *that's the way we've always done it* often results in an outdated value stream that contains unnecessary or inefficient steps and processes.

NOTE

There should be an identifiable and legitimate reason for each step in a company's value stream and how it is performed.

Mapping the Value Stream

Companies can optimize their value stream to eliminate unnecessary steps and improve inefficient ones. First, though, they must identify those steps. This involves a process called *mapping*.

Mapping the value stream for a product or feature involves assembling a team of representatives from each functional group that contributes to the value stream: product, design, development, QA, infosec, operations, and so on. Each representative then details all the specific steps their group takes to deliver the product or feature.

The resulting value-stream map should include every step taken, no matter how small, to deliver the product or feature from start to finish. It should also note:

- How long each step takes
- Which team or person is responsible for each step
- Which steps are performed manually and which are automated
- What tools are used to complete each step
- Which steps require approval and by whom
- Where handoffs occur

Mapping the value stream is always an eye-opener. It's usually the first time everyone sees just how much work goes into a product or feature. It's also usually the first time members of different groups grasp how their work affects others—particularly those downstream.

Value-stream mapping is a big job. It takes a lot of time and effort. Not surprisingly, a lot of companies put it off or ignore it altogether. But value-stream mapping is critical. It's the only way to expose all the waste in a system.

NOTE

There's no such thing as a perfect value stream—and even if there were, some condition would inevitably change to disrupt it. When it comes to value streams, there's *always* room for improvement!

Value-stream mapping can also reveal another problem: bottlenecks. Recall that a *bottleneck* is any step that clogs the value stream, hinders workflow, and prolongs the development cycle. Bottlenecks often occur in the form of setup time, queue time, or wait time. (See the upcoming sidebar "The Four Types of Time in a Production Line," for more information on each of these.)

The Four Types of Time in a Production Line

Experts have identified four types of time in any production line, including the software development life cycle:

- **SETUP:** The time a piece of work spends waiting for a resource (person or machine) to be set up to complete it. An example of setup time in the context of software development might be time spent waiting for a development environment to be provisioned.

- **PROCESS:** The time a resource spends actually working on the piece of work.

- **QUEUE:** The time a piece of work spends waiting for a resource to finish something else before starting the piece of work.

- **WAIT:** The time a piece of work spends waiting for some other piece of work to be completed so the two pieces of work can be assembled together.

Obviously, the idea in any production system is to minimize process time and to eliminate setup, queue, and wait time (also called *wait conditions*).

The following sections discuss ways to wipe out waste and elimi-nate bottlenecks to optimize the value stream. They also cover other techniques: prioritizing important work and making work visible.

Wiping Out Waste

Mapping the value stream helps identify waste in the form of unneces-sary or inefficient steps. But how do companies eliminate this waste? Simple. They remove unnecessary steps and improve inefficient ones.

Companies improve inefficient steps by locating and removing any gates in their value stream. A *gate* is anything that results in a wait con-dition—in other words, setup time, queue time, or wait time. Examples of gates include:

- HANDOFFS: A *handoff* is when one team turns a piece of work over to another team. Handoffs require a flurry of communica-tion in the form of meetings, phone calls, texts, email messages, or IMs to coordinate, schedule, and prioritize, which bleed time. Handoffs also result in a loss of knowledge—sometimes so much that employees "completely lose the context of the problem being solved or the organizational goal being supported," say the authors of *The DevOps Handbook*. Companies can limit handoffs by keeping more tasks within a single team or automating tasks.

- HEAVY-HANDED INSPECTION AND APPROVAL PROCESSES: Inspection and approval processes such as change management boards are often overkill. Generally, companies can scale down these processes or make them more efficient by ensuring that they are completed by people who are close to the work being evaluated. Even better, they can automate many of these processes.

NOTE

Implementing small cross-functional teams helps eliminate gates.

Other Forms of Waste in the
Software Development Life Cycle

Needless or inefficient steps are just one type of waste in the software development life cycle. Here are a few others:

- UNWANTED FEATURES: Any feature that your customers don't want are waste.

- MULTITASKING: Studies show that switching between tasks makes *all* your tasks take longer.

- WAITING: Idle time is wasted time.

- MOTION: The time and effort required to move information or materials to another person or location is often considered waste.

- DEFECTS: In the context of software development, a *defect* is information, materials, or products that are incorrect, missing, or unclear.

- MANUAL WORK: Tasks that could be automated but aren't are waste, as are nonstandard tasks.

- PARTIALLY COMPLETED WORK: The longer work sits uncompleted, the less value it retains, until eventually it has no value at all.

- HEROICS: Forcing employees to do work equivalent to lifting a car off a person just to finish their daily tasks saps them of their energy.

Wiping out these types of waste can also help maximize flow, not to mention reduce "hardship and drudgery in our daily work," say the authors of *The DevOps Handbook*.

Eliminating Bottlenecks

As mentioned, a bottleneck (also called a *constraint*) is any step that takes so long to complete that it clogs the value stream, hinders workflow, and prolongs the development cycle. A bottleneck forms when, for whatever reason, the person, team, or tool responsible for completing a step doesn't have what it needs to do it in a timely fashion. (See Figure 3.2.)

FIGURE 3.2 The bottleneck shown here limits how many ducks can cross from one pond to the other at once.

Several steps in the software development life cycle commonly cause bottlenecks, particularly in non-DevOps shops:

- ENVIRONMENT PROVISIONING: Many organizations require the operations team to manually provision environments. This process can take weeks or even months.

- COMPUTATIONS: Computational bottlenecks arise when companies don't have enough compute power to handle the workload.

- APPROVAL PROCESSES: Work that must be inspected and approved before advancing to the next phase adds significant time.

- TESTING: Conducting manual QA and security tests late in the development process can result in a jam.

- DEPLOYMENTS: Cumbersome manual deployment routines often cause backups.

NOTE

Manual tasks are often to blame for bottlenecks.

Identifying and eliminating bottlenecks in the value stream is one obvious way to maximize flow. In fact, according to Lean, it's the *only* way. As noted in Chapter 2, Lean calls for system improvements at the bottleneck and *only* the bottleneck because:

- System improvements made *before* the bottleneck only create a bigger clog at the bottleneck.

- System improvements made *after* the bottleneck just starve downstream groups of work.

Identifying and eliminating bottlenecks to maximize flow is based on the *Theory of Constraints*, a managerial philosophy devised by renowned business management expert Dr. Eliyahu M. Goldratt. The Theory of Constraints dictates that organizations focus on the bottleneck (constraint) at the expense of all other improvements until that bottleneck is eliminated and a new bottleneck is identified.

NOTE

Dr. Goldratt's Theory of Constraints revolutionized the way manufacturing companies—and software companies—operate.

Dr. Goldratt identifies five steps to eliminating bottlenecks:

1. Identify the system's bottleneck.
2. Exploit the bottleneck by ensuring that it always operates at full capacity.
3. Prioritize the improvement of the bottleneck above all else.
4. Apply resources to elevate the bottleneck's performance.
5. When the bottleneck is eliminated, repeat steps 1–4 for the next bottleneck.

CAUTION

Dr. Goldratt warns against the dangers of inertia. When inertia sets in —and it will—*it* can become your system's bottleneck!

What does it mean to apply resources to elevate the bottleneck's performance? Well, this could involve:

- Hiring new employees to address the volume of work at the bottleneck
- Training existing employees to jump in to help when work backs up at the bottleneck
- Purchasing tools to expedite or even automate the work at the bottleneck

Companies might also be able to eliminate the bottleneck simply by wiping out waste within the step or process that's causing it.

It might be impossible to eliminate a bottleneck *completely*. In that case, it's best to divert downstream groups to other tasks until the work at the bottleneck makes its way to them. Those other tasks can include learning a new skill, experimenting with a new technology, or paying down technical debt. (You'll learn more about technical debt later in this chapter.)

Prioritizing Important Work

President Dwight D. Eisenhower once said, "I have two kinds of problems: the urgent and the important. The urgent are not important, and the important are never urgent." Steven Covey, who wrote *The 7 Habits of Highly Effective People,* tweaked this idea to create something he called the Eisenhower Decision Matrix.

The Eisenhower Decision Matrix divided work into four categories:

- URGENT AND IMPORTANT: This includes crises of all kinds as well as certain critical deadlines. Do work that is both urgent and important immediately.

- NOT URGENT BUT IMPORTANT: This includes any work that pertains to success over the long term—training, preventive work, or even relationship-building, for example. You should schedule time to do this type of work.

- URGENT BUT NOT IMPORTANT: This work requires immediate attention but does not further your long-term goals. An example is a meeting or a phone call on a topic that's outside your purview. Defer or delegate this type of work if you can.

- NOT URGENT AND NOT IMPORTANT: This is busywork. Don't do it, and don't ask anyone else to, either.

NOTE

Crises means real emergencies—things like "We might go out of business if we don't fix this problem immediately," not "This icon needs to be *cornflower* blue, not *sky* blue."

Making Work Visible

To ensure work flows smoothly through the value stream, everyone should be able to see the status of each step in the stream. This helps prevent waste in the form of waiting or heroics.

There are a few good ways to make work visible:

- Dashboards
- Internal websites
- Kanban boards

Dashboards and internal websites are pretty self-explanatory. These tools keep everyone apprised of the work's progress in the value stream.

The third option requires a bit more explanation. A *Kanban board* contains columns for each stage of the value stream and cards for each task to be completed. When someone finishes a task, they move its card to the next column on the board to show its progress.

NOTE

A Kanban board could be a physical board or a software application.

In addition to these options, teams in DevOps shops often conduct scrums to help make their work visible. A *scrum* is a daily team meeting that usually occurs in the morning. During the scrum, each team member updates everyone else on what they did yesterday, what they plan to do today, and, if applicable, any obstacles in their way.

Applying Continuous Delivery

Once you understand the value stream, a practice called *continuous delivery* can help you improve it to maximize flow. *Continuous delivery* (*CD*) is a software engineering approach that automates and shortens the software delivery process.

CD differs from the waterfall model in another critical way, too. With CD, instead of deploying software all at once, at the tail end of the development cycle, code is kept in a deployable state throughout the entire development cycle and can be safely released anytime.

To keep code in a continuously deployable state, teams must adhere to a few key practices. (You'll learn more about each of these practices in a moment.)

- Doing continuous integration
- Using an automated deployment pipeline
- Automating common and repetitive tasks
- Taking advantage of tools

NOTE

CD also requires constant monitoring and feedback. This is covered in Chapter 4, "Obtaining Fast Feedback."

CD can have a hugely positive impact on your organization. But, the authors of *Accelerate: The Science of Lean Software and DevOps* say, "implementing these practices often requires rethinking everything—from how teams work, to how they interact with each other, to what tools and processes they use." So, be ready for that!

NOTE

People often confuse continuous delivery with another common DevOps practice: continuous deployment (also abbreviated as CD). Here's the difference: *Continuous delivery* means having the ability to deploy anytime, while *continuous deployment* means automating the actual deployment process. (You'll learn more about continuous deployment in a moment.)

Doing Continuous Integration

With waterfall, developers might work for weeks or even months on a piece of code before committing it to the larger codebase. By the time the code is finally committed, it's large and unwieldy, and inevitably causes conflicts and other problems.

Continuous integration (CI) takes a different approach. With CI, developers commit small batches of code on a near-continuous basis—

at least once a day, and maybe more often than that. So, the codebase is always as up to date as possible.

NOTE

In organizations with developers numbering in the dozens or hundreds, code could be updated hundreds or even thousands of times per day.

Continuously committing small batches of code offers several critical benefits:

- It eliminates bottlenecks.
- It supports an experimental and iterative approach.
- It facilitates faster feedback.
- It allows quicker fixes.
- It reduces rework.
- It eases deployments.
- It improves agility.

NOTE

CI evolved from Agile and is an important DevOps practice.

Achieving CI involves three key practices:

- Build automation
- Version control
- Automated testing for security and quality

BUILD AUTOMATION

Complex software products usually involve an equally complicated build process. Often, this process becomes even more convoluted and inefficient over time with the addition of modules and procedures.

A build process that requires frequent human intervention is especially problematic. In addition to diverting staff attention, it competes for computational resources during regular working hours (among other issues).

Automating the build process solves these problems. Build automation frees staff to focus on more critical and interesting tasks. It also frees computational resources during work hours because unattended build processes can be run during off-hours.

Before automating the build process, companies must analyze the existing build environment to identify the following:

- All entities involved in the build process, including staff, tools, and more
- All procedures, manual and otherwise
- Bottlenecks
- Inconsistencies
- Manual steps
- Inefficient steps
- Hazardous steps

Then, companies can make changes to eliminate bottlenecks, inconsistencies, and manual, inefficient, and hazardous steps. These changes could include, but are not limited to:

- Developing new scripts and wrappers to tie separate build phases together or to replace manual procedures
- Revamping existing scripts
- Reorganizing the build sequence and resource use
- Improving build logging processes to support troubleshooting and recordkeeping
- Sending automatic notification emails to appropriate individuals about the build status

NOTE
Build automation is one of the keys to CI.

VERSION CONTROL
Recall that CI involves committing small batches of code on a near-continuous basis. Each time this happens, the system saves a new version

of the codebase along with information about who initiated the commit and when. This process is called *version control*.

With version control, there's no confusion as to which version of the product or feature is the most up to date. Version control acts as a single source of truth and provides an audit history for verifying compliance. Version control also makes it easy to roll back the product or feature to a more stable version if a developer commits a piece of code that doesn't work well with other pieces. Changes are visible, allowing team members to help if a commit goes awry.

NOTE
Version control is one of the foundations of solid software development.

Trunk-Based Development

Software projects are often described using a tree metaphor, with the tree trunk containing all pieces of the project that are complete and stable, and the branches supporting everything that is in progress.

A complex project might have dozens or even hundreds of branches. Merge conflicts can make committing changes to the codebase difficult and time-consuming.

Some smaller teams address this problem by using an approach called *trunk-based development* (*TBD*). With TBD, the team focuses its work on a single branch. This helps prevent the problems associated with committing changes to the codebase.

This is a good methodology for simpler projects. However, as projects grow, teams will likely soon find the need to create additional branches for various features, releases, and bug fixes.

AUTOMATED TESTING FOR SECURITY AND QUALITY
CI requires automated testing for quality and security. Manual tests just can't keep up. Automatic tests can be configured to run on demand or to launch by default anytime a developer commits code.

The exact nature of these tests will vary depending on the product or feature under development. Still, the objective of each test is the same: to verify that the code works as intended, and to identify quality or security concerns so the developer can address them immediately. Automated tests that ensure security compliance also make it easier to respond to requests from auditors or assessors if a problem arises down the line.

NOTE
For more on automated testing, see Chapter 4.

Using an Automated Deployment Pipeline

Although the DevOps workflow can be described in waterfall terms, DevOps practitioners generally think of it as a pipeline. This pipeline—called the *deployment pipeline*—is a manifestation of an organization's value-stream map.

The deployment pipeline is more than just a model. It's a series of tools, many of which are automated, that ensures that code remains in a continuously deployable state. These include tools for build automation, version control, and automated testing, as well as for the following activities:

- Automatic provisioning of production-like environments
- Continuous deployment

Together, these tools enable developers to quickly and continuously:

- Introduce changes to code
- Keep track of those changes
- Ensure changes do not negatively affect the quality or security of the feature or product
- Deploy changes automatically

AUTOMATIC PROVISIONING OF PRODUCTION-LIKE ENVIRONMENTS

In many organizations, developers must wait for a member of the IT function to provision a development or test environment for them. This can take days or even weeks and create a significant bottleneck.

Complicating matters is the fact that in many organizations, the environment that is eventually provisioned does not mirror a production environment. In these cases, performance problems and other issues go undetected until the code is deployed.

Automatic provisioning solves these problems by:

- Supporting automatic and on-demand environment provisioning
- Ensuring all environments mirror the production environment—even environments used early on by developers on their own workstations

Automatic and on-demand environment provision often occurs via third-party cloud providers. These providers enable developers to simply spool up environments as needed and release them when they're finished. Provisioning code this way is an example of *infrastructure as code*. Infrastructure as code isn't just faster; it's also more cost-effective, because companies pay for only the resources they use. It also enables them to ensure consistency and security across environments.

Virtual machines (VMs) and containers are two common tools for provisioning development environments on demand. A *VM* is software that emulates a computer and is often accessed via a network or the cloud. A *container* is a standard unit of software that packages code for an application and all its dependencies so it can run quickly and reliably from one computing environment to another.

NOTE

An in-depth discussion of VMs and containers is outside the scope of this book.

CONTINUOUS DEPLOYMENT

Continuous delivery keeps code in a deployable state throughout the development cycle—meaning companies can automate the deployment process. Anyone can launch an automated deployment process—not just someone in ops—with the click of a button. Or, a deployment could start automatically anytime a developer commits code. This is called *continuous deployment*.

Cloud Computing

Cloud computing involves using a network of remote servers rather than a local server to store, manage, and process data. This network is called the *cloud*.

Resources available from the cloud include:

- SOFTWARE AS A SERVICE (SAAS): SaaS is a software delivery model in which customers access and use software online instead of installing it on their own computers.

- PLATFORM AS A SERVICE (PAAS): PaaS is like SaaS, but instead of accessing and using software online, customers access and use platforms and tools to develop, deploy, and manage software products.

- INFRASTRUCTURE AS A SERVICE (IAAS): With IaaS, third-party providers host servers, storage, and other compute resources for customer use. Companies use IaaS to avoid the overhead associated with building and maintaining their own infrastructure.

Using cloud services allows "faster innovation, flexible resources, and economies of scale," says Emily Freeman. Additionally, "you typically pay only for cloud services you use, which helps you lower your operating costs, run your infrastructure more efficiently, and scale as your business needs change."

Continuous deployment represents an enormous change from the death march deployments so common in traditional organizations. Continuous deployments are quick and easy, and unlike deployments under waterfall—which typically occur on nights or weekends—they happen during normal working hours.

Failing Forward

After a failure, rolling back the system to determine what went wrong is often the safest response. However, it might not be the *right* response. Instead, it might make more sense to fail forward—that is, to fix the problem *without* rolling things back. This usually results in a quicker fix.

Deployment Versus Release

Deploying is not the same as releasing, although the two words are often used interchangeably. To *deploy* is to deliver to a production environment the code for a feature, set of features, or product. To *release* is to make that feature, set of features, or product available to some or all of your customers.

When deployments occur only infrequently, they dictate how quickly software can be released. With continuous deployment, "how quickly we expose new functionality to customers becomes a business and marketing decision, not a technical one," say the authors of *The DevOps Handbook*. That's a good thing.

On a related note: Although companies certainly can release new software to all their customers at once, they don't have to. Instead, they can release it to smaller or select groups of customers before rolling it out to a wider audience. This gives companies a chance to test things out, solicit feedback, and minimize the likelihood of outages.

Automating Common and Repetitive Tasks

If companies want their developers to commit and perhaps even deploy code every day, they need to relieve them of tasks that machines can perform just as well (or perhaps even better). In other words, they need to automate these tasks.

In addition to freeing developers to produce at a breakneck pace, automating common and repetitive tasks helps prevent human errors. It also gives teams the bandwidth they need to pay down technical debt, which further speeds up the development cycle. And, as discussed, it can maximize flow.

As mentioned, companies can automate tasks that pertain to environment provisioning, testing, and code deploying—but these are just a few examples of tasks that can be automated. The truth is, companies can automate tasks throughout the deployment pipeline, like generating builds, packaging, archiving, reporting, staging, releasing, and more.

Technical Debt

Technical debt describes the long-term price of short-term decisions like taking shortcuts or putting off planned or preventive work.

Suppose you were planning to spend the day completing some code for an important project, but your boss pulls you in to deal with a problem downstream. You resolve the issue, but now you're behind in your coding work. Facing an impossible deadline, you take some shortcuts with your code. These shortcuts create even more problems downstream, which you are pulled in to solve, putting you even further behind in your regular work. This misspent time is an example of technical debt.

Technical debt is like financial debt. When you take on too much, you can find yourself drowning in it, paying off only the interest and accruing even *more* technical debt. Eventually, you get to the point that you have so much technical debt, you never complete any new work.

Before automating any process, companies must be certain the process is solid. In *DevOps For Dummies*, Emily Freeman observes that "automating a failure-ridden process only helps you fail more spectacularly and abstract the source of the failure."

NOTE

DevOps requires automation.

Taking Advantage of Tools

DevOps in general, and CI and CD in particular, rely heavily on tools to maximize flow. Table 3.1 lists categories of tools for use in DevOps. (Appendix B lists specific tools in each category.)

TABLE 3.1   DevOps Tool Categories

Category	Description
Frameworks and libraries	Frameworks and libraries enable developers to plug in existing approved code for common operations so they don't reinvent the wheel.
Collaboration	Collaboration tools enable geographically separate teams to share information, provide feedback, eliminate ineffective handoff procedures, and track issues. These tools are designed to replace more traditional forms of communication.
Project management	Project management tools enable leaders and product owners to establish strategies, develop roadmaps, and decompose requirements into individual tasks. They can also prioritize, assign, and schedule tasks, and use time management tools for reporting purposes.
Requirements management	Requirements management tools enable teams to record new requests and decompose them into individual tasks.
Source code management (SCM) and version control	SCM and version control tools store source code in a repository and allow for automatic version control, change tracking, audit history, and documentation storage.
SCM clients	Using local SCM clients (rather than cloud-based repositories) enables team members to work on the same codebase from their own local machines.
Database automation	Database automation tools allow unattended processes and self-updating procedures to perform administrative database tasks.
Asset management	Asset management tools enable teams to reuse items during the development stage to ensure their code contains everything needed for each build.
Testing	Testing tools enable teams to capture code execution and user operations, use these to create a test case, and automate the entire test cycle from within the application.
Code review	Code review tools expedite the code review process to ensure fast feedback.

(continues...)

TABLE 3.1 DevOps Tool Categories (continued)

Category	Description
Build management and automation	Build management and automation tools are what developers use to compile code changes prior to release. During the build process, scripts perform such tasks as generating documentation, executing previously defined tests, compiling the code, and distributing related binaries.
Continuous integration (CI)	Continuous integration tools enable teams to automate version control and change tracking and to trigger builds and tests. They may also include features for automatic deployment.
Release orchestration	With release management tools, teams can orchestrate releases across different tools, environments, and teams.
Continuous delivery (CD) and continuous deployment (CD)	Continuous delivery and continuous deployment tools constantly conduct automated QA and infosec tests and commit code. The deployment process can also be automated to pull software into production as soon as it passes all automated checks.
Configuration management	Configuration management tools automate process management tasks such as identifying tasks, tools, documents, equipment, and components, and managing related revisions or versions.
Infrastructure as code	Infrastructure as code tools allow for the automatic provisioning of resources.
Virtual machines (VMs) and containers	Virtual machines (VMs) and containers allow for the use of containers to create lightweight applications.
Cloud	Cloud tools enable geographically separate teams to create, test, release, and monitor software without compromising code integrity and provide added automation capabilities.
Change management	Change management tools provide formal approval workflows for new code and store the audit history of each change.
Incident management	Incident management tools capture and report issues. They can also categorize issues and route information about an issue to relevant teams.
Issue tracking	Issue tracking tools find, record, and track bugs and defects.

Analytics	Analytics tools deliver actionable information such as test pass rates, build stability, bug tracking, and defect logging. These provide insight into such areas as team performance, task processing, release cycles and frequencies, and compliance with development processes.
Security	Teams can use security tools to detect and alert developers of suspicious code and to identify weaknesses and flaws.
IT service management (ITSM)	ITSM tools ensure regulatory compliance and system security.
Tool suites and centralized tool management	Tool suites offer all (or several) of the tools you need for the entire deployment pipeline. Tools in a suite are designed to work together for maximum efficiency. (Whether a company opts for a complete tool suite or assembles a combination of tools from different vendors often depends on their budget.) For organizations that choose not to use a tool suite, a centralized tool management solution can help ensure the various tools work well together.

NOTE

Tools are important, but culture is more so. A company could buy literally every tool for DevOps ever built, but if the culture is toxic, their DevOps effort will fail. Still, there are lots of tools that can help companies that already have positive learning cultures implement DevOps.

Companies that adopt a DevOps approach will likely need to invest in tools. Here are a few suggestions to keep in mind:

- USE TOOLS THAT WORK: Choose the tool (or suite) that fits your process. Don't change your process to fit the tool!

- CHOOSE TOOLS THAT ARE FLEXIBLE AND RESILIENT: Don't choose those that lock you into using them a certain way.

- AVOID VENDOR LOCK-IN: *Vendor lock-in* describes when a company has invested so much in tools from one vendor that switching to another, better vendor becomes cost-prohibitive.

- LOOK TO THE CLOUD: Some companies offer cloud-based tools. These tools can offer several advantages, ranging from cost and speed to scalability.

- CONSIDER OPEN SOURCE TOOLS: Many companies offer open source tools for use in a deployment pipeline. Open source tools are inexpensive or free, well-engineered, and easily modified. However, they might be hard to integrate and maintain, and usually offer little support.

- ALLOW TEAMS TO HELP SELECT TOOLS: If possible, companies should let teams choose the tools they prefer. This will likely improve productivity *and* grant teams a sense of autonomy.

NOTE

In larger companies, it might be easier and more cost-effective for the entire organization to use the same toolset rather than allowing teams to pick their own. Businesses must weigh the value of potentially having more productive teams against the costs associated with maintaining multiple tools per category (including training, licensing, hosting, and so on).

To quote Emily Freeman, "The tools you select should solve the problems your engineering team experiences, but should also align with the style, knowledge, and comfort areas of your existing team." Tools should also "be useful, easy to use, and provide users with the right information," says DevOps expert Nicole Forsgren.

Practicing Continuous Improvement

Successful DevOps shops don't rest on their laurels. They practice continuous improvement, constantly evaluating their value stream to identify areas for improvement. These improvements might be incremental—little changes that add up over time—or they might be breakthrough improvements that happen all at once. Identifying new and more efficient ways of working helps maximize flow.

One way to practice continuous improvement is to employ a model called the *improvement kata*, popularized by Mike Rother. This model involves five key steps:

1. UNDERSTANDING THE DIRECTION: This is usually based on some insight uncovered by the value stream–mapping exercise and articulated by company leadership. The direction should be inspiring—maybe even a bit of a stretch.

2. GRASPING THE CURRENT CONDITION: Assess how a particular process that relates to the articulated direction stands right now.

3. ESTABLISHING THE NEXT TARGET CONDITION: The target condition describes how the process should be in the future.

4. ITERATING TOWARD THE TARGET CONDITION: Take steps to improve the process so it aligns more closely with the articulated direction.

5. REPEATING STEPS 2–4: Do it again *ad infinitum*.

NOTE

Continuous improvement never ends. There's *always* room to improve.

What specific steps should companies take to improve a process? Here are a few ideas:

- CONDUCT IMPROVEMENT BLITZES OR HACKATHONS: Assemble a small group of people to focus exclusively on a specific problem over a period of days.

- PERFORM PREVENTIVE WORK: Just as cars require occasional tune-ups, so do value streams. Preventive work reduces technical debt and unplanned work (think *firefighting*) down the line.

- ELIMINATE TECHNICAL DEBT: Often, cumbersome, time-consuming workarounds are the price of technical debt. Paying down this debt by improving processes in which it has accrued can bring significant gains.

TIP

Some percentage of each blitz should involve attacking technical debt. Attacking technical debt is also a good way to ramp up developers who are new to a team.

In addition to processes, continuous improvement also means continuously improving offered products and features, particularly in the following areas:

- Maintainability
- Scalability
- Security
- Usability
- Reliability
- Flexibility

NOTE

Processes and products should be living documents, like the United States' Constitution. They should evolve over time as the company's needs, and its customers' needs, change.

Conclusion

Maximizing flow is one of the three keys to DevOps. Companies can maximize flow by:

- Moving downstream groups upstream to form small, cross-functional teams
- Optimizing the value stream by wiping out waste, eliminating bottlenecks, prioritizing important work, and making work visible
- Applying continuous delivery by practicing continuous integration and automating the deployment pipeline
- Practicing continuous improvement

The next chapter explores the second key to DevOps: obtaining fast feedback.

4

Obtaining Fast Feedback

"We all need people who will give us feedback. That's how we improve."

–Bill Gates

In This Chapter:

- Shortening Feedback Loops
- Automating Testing
- Using Telemetry
- Obtaining Feedback from Peers and Downstream Groups
- Soliciting Customer Feedback

Companies that obtain fast feedback can ensure they're building a product or feature that people want, and that they're doing it in the most efficient way.

Fast feedback offers many benefits:

- Increased learning
- Faster failures and fixes
- Lower failure rates
- Improved quality and security
- Easier deployments
- Increased agility
- Higher levels of customer satisfaction

Obtaining fast feedback also satisfies two of Gene Kim's Five Ideals: improvement of daily work and customer focus.

Companies obtain fast feedback by shortening feedback loops from various sources. This chapter covers these feedback sources and discusses what companies can do with feedback once they get it.

Shortening Feedback Loops

Feedback enables companies to ensure they're working on the right things in the right way. But if they don't obtain feedback in a timely manner—that is, while they can still act on or at least learn from it—it's essentially worthless.

As discussed in Chapter 1, "Before DevOps," long feedback loops like those in waterfall systems do not allow for timely feedback. Consider:

- The feedback loop from the QA and infosec teams to the design and development teams might span six months or even one year.
- The feedback loop from the operations team to the design and development teams will be even longer.
- The feedback loop from customers to the product and design teams will be longer still.

By the time the designers and developers who worked on a product or feature finally receive feedback from downstream groups, odds are they will have long forgotten how they designed and built the product or feature and why they did it that way. This drastically reduces the likelihood of learning from the feedback, let alone a quick (or even any) fix. And by the time *customer* feedback finally rolls in? Well, that will be long after the product and design groups can cheaply and easily adapt it or scrap it.

Short feedback loops solve these problems. Companies can implement short feedback loops from peers and downstream functions to product, design, and development groups to provide feedback in a matter of days or even minutes rather than months or years. Companies can also implement short feedback loops to obtain customer feedback on new features and products early in the development cycle so they can change or chuck them that much faster.

In addition to enabling companies to adapt, short feedback loops allow them to fail fast. For example, short feedback loops from operations to development prevent developers from sending code down the pipeline that's impossible to deploy. Similarly, short feedback loops from customers to the product group keep companies from sinking months or even years of work (not to mention millions of dollars) into a new product or feature only to find out it's a lemon after it's released.

NOTE

In a waterfall system, the earliest indication of a problem often occurs when a catastrophic event is already underway. Short feedback loops help surface problems sooner, *before* they become catastrophes.

Automating Testing

You already know that automating quality and security testing maximizes flow. But the *way* it maximizes flow is by providing fast—in some cases, immediate—feedback to developers. This enables developers to:

- Ensure that code remains in a deployable state.
- Find and fix problems right away.
- Learn to avoid similar problems in the future.

There are several types of automatic tests to evaluate quality and security:

- UNIT TESTS: These assess a single piece of code—that is, a method, class, or function—within a component to confirm that it operates as expected. Unit tests typically take milliseconds to complete. Developers should run a unit test each time they commit code.

- ACCEPTANCE TESTS: These evaluate how a component works as a whole. Acceptance tests typically take a few seconds to complete. Like unit tests, developers should run an acceptance test each time they commit code.

- INTEGRATION TESTS: These ensure that a component works well with other components in the product. They usually take a few minutes to complete. Developers should run an integration test each time they commit code.

- PERFORMANCE TESTS: These assess the performance of a component within a product or the product as a whole. Ideally, developers should run a performance test each time they commit code. This might not be feasible, however, because these tests sometimes take hours or days to complete. In that case, the tests should be run nightly or weekly (schedule and resources permitting).

- REGRESSION TESTS: These ensure that changes made to code don't introduce errors, bugs, or other problems. The duration of a regression test depends on how much code is affected by the change, with a full regression test taking weeks or months to complete. Obviously, regression tests are not performed as often as other tests, but they should still be run on a regular basis.

NOTE

The more developers a company has, the more important automatic testing becomes, because it helps ensure the code's integrity—even when developers enter thousands of commits per day.

Developers at Google run hundreds of thousands of automated tests each time they commit code. Although most companies probably don't need *that* many, they do need an across-the-board arsenal of automated tests. One way companies assemble this arsenal is by providing developers with the tools and the time to write tests that assess their code as they work. As developers write more and more tests, the automated testing suite becomes more and more powerful. (Of course, it is also possible to purchase testing software.)

TIP

Companies should give developers the tools they need to write and run tests at their own workstations. For more information on tools, see Appendix B, "Tools for DevOps Success."

Automated testing might not completely eliminate manual tests, especially at first. But in general, the more tests a company can automate, the better—unless, of course, those tests are unreliable or useless. It is better to have a few good tests than a battery of checks that are undependable or deliver unnecessary information!

TIP

To find errors earlier rather than later, companies run faster tests before slower tests, and run automated tests before manual ones.

Using Telemetry

Telemetry, or using instrumentation to collect data, is another useful form of automated feedback. DevOps promotes telemetry for monitoring and logging the behavior or performance of:

- Each component in a product
- A product as a whole
- Infrastructure components
- Processes in the deployment pipeline
- Employees
- Customers

NOTE

If a process or feature was important enough to build and implement, it's important enough to monitor by telemetry.

Telemetry offers several benefits:

- It acts as an early warning system for emerging problems.
- It reveals the source of a problem, so teams can solve it much faster—ideally before the customer even notices it.
- It conveys an accurate view to everyone in the value stream.
- It reveals areas for improvement.
- It informs business decisions.

TIP

Just as you can empower developers to write their own automated tests, you can—and should—empower them to set up their own code for telemetry.

The trick to telemetry is to track the right metrics. These might vary from project to project. Here are some examples of metrics a company might consider.

- LEAD TIME: How long it takes to start on a product or feature.
- DEPLOYMENT FREQUENCY AND SIZE: How often deployments occur, and how large they are. It's best to have frequent small deployments.
- DEPLOYMENT LENGTH: The time it takes to complete the deployment process.
- FAILED DEPLOYMENTS: The number of times a deployment operation has failed.
- DEFECT ESCAPE RATE: The number of defects that should have been detected before deployment but weren't.
- ERROR RATE: The number of errors found after deployment.
- RECURRING FAILURE RATE: The number of errors that occurred more than once after deployment.
- CHANGE FAILURE RATE: A ratio that compares the total number of failures with the number of changes introduced.
- MEAN TIME TO DETECTION (MTTD): The time from the moment a problem begins affecting customers and the moment the company detects the problem.
- MEAN TIME TO RECOVERY (MTTR): The time from the moment a problem begins affecting customers and the moment the company fixes the problem.
- AUTOMATED TEST COVERAGE: The percentage of automated tests used in the development of a product or feature.
- ATTEMPTED SECURITY BREACHES: How many times a security breach was attempted.

- SUCCESSFUL SECURITY BREACHES: How many times a security breach was successful.

- AVAILABILITY: The product uptime.

- CUSTOMER USAGE: How many customers are using the product and how they are using it.

- CUSTOMER TRAFFIC: Where customers are using the product and how many times.

- FREQUENCY OF CUSTOMER VISITS: How often each person uses the product.

- NUMBER OF CUSTOMER TICKETS: How many issues customers have flagged with the product.

Once companies decide what metrics to track, they can configure the telemetry to send alerts when a given metric falls outside an acceptable range.

A company's approach to telemetry is likely to evolve over time. At first, companies typically focus on establishing baselines for each metric they choose. Later, they might add new metrics. For example, if a product experiences some type of problem or failure, the company might devise a new metric to prevent it from happening again—for example, by detecting a different or even weaker failure signal.

When it comes to metrics, companies should heed these warnings:

- STEER CLEAR OF VANITY METRICS: A *vanity metric* is "a piece of data on which you cannot act," say Alistair Croll and Benjamin Yoskovitz.

- AVOID OVER- AND UNDER-ALERTING: To *over-alert* is to flag events that aren't a concern. Over-alerting induces alert fatigue. When people have alert fatigue, they start ignoring all alerts—even those they should respond to. To *under-alert* is to fail to flag events that *are* cause for concern. To borrow from Goldilocks, alerting should be "just right."

- DON'T USE METRICS TO REWARD EMPLOYEES: They will game the system to work in their favor.

- DON'T USE METRICS TO PUNISH EMPLOYEES: This will encourage them to cover up problems.

NOTE

Metrics should serve as a point of reference and offer insights to help companies improve. That's all.

Obtaining Feedback from Peers and Downstream Groups

Shortening the feedback loop between downstream groups and the development team can have a powerful effect on the quality and security of the product or feature under development, as well as on the process by which that product or feature is built.

Although it is not necessarily easy, one simple way to shorten this feedback loop is to organize all these functions—development, QA, infosec, and operations (and perhaps even upstream functions like design and product)—into small cross-functional teams. This practice is called *shifting left*. As noted in Chapter 3, "Maximizing Flow," shifting downstream groups left offers these advantages:

- Downstream groups can weigh in on the product or feature during the development process rather than after it. This enables them to spot quality and security problems early on.

- Downstream groups can ensure that the product or feature is engineered with their concerns in mind, with features like quality, privacy, security, maintainability, and so on, built-in.

With small cross-functional teams, some of this feedback occurs naturally. For example, an infosec specialist might share concerns about a feature with a developer at the water cooler. Or an ops staffer could mention a glitch to a developer while perusing goodies in the canteen.

TIP

Negative feedback is easier to hear when it comes from a trusted source. Small cross-functional teams facilitate this.

Other feedback might involve more formal processes, such as meetings attended by members of different functional groups. (Of course, these types of meetings are effective even if members of functional teams *aren't* organized into small cross-functional teams.)

Tools like bug- and issue-tracking software can facilitate fast feedback from downstream groups. For more on these, see Appendix B, "Tools for DevOps Success."

Feedback from peers is also important. This type of feedback can help prevent errors and facilitate learning. Code reviews are one example of this type of feedback. A *code review* involves one developer examining another's work either immediately before the code is committed or immediately after.

Here are a few ways to conduct code reviews:

- PAIR PROGRAMMING: Two developers pair at a single workstation. As one developer writes code, the other reviews it. This occurs before the code is committed.

- OVER-THE-SHOULDER: After finishing writing a piece of code, the developer walks another developer through it. This occurs before the code is committed.

- VIA EMAIL: When one developer commits code, the system automatically emails designated peers to instruct them to review it.

- WITHIN THE CODEBASE: After one developer commits code, other developers add comments directly in the codebase (assuming the codebase supports this functionality).

It's a good practice for everyone on the team to monitor the commit stream to identify potential conflicts.

Code reviews offer several benefits:

- Fewer errors in the code
- A sense of shared ownership among team members
- A chance to question assumptions
- Coaching for less-experienced programmers
- An opportunity for senior engineers to stay on top of the code
- Exposure to more aspects of the codebase
- A more unified codebase

TIP

Appendix B lists some tools for use in code reviews.

A retrospective is another example of peer feedback—although this happens at the end of the development cycle. A *retrospective* is a meeting in which the team discusses what was successful about the development cycle, what could have been improved, and how to repeat the successes and incorporate the improvements in the future.

The Real Price of Craptastic Ideas

Developing products or features that customers don't notice or that actively upset them is bad. It's also expensive. First, there are the costs associated with developing the product or feature. Then there are the expenses involved with maintaining the code. Finally, there are the *opportunity costs*, which are incurred by *not* developing a product or feature that people actually want to use. All that adds up!

Soliciting Customer Feedback

Feedback from automated tests, telemetry, downstream groups, and peers can tell companies whether they're using the right processes. But feedback from customers can tell them if they're building the right thing.

Recall from Chapter 1 that between 60 and 90 percent of ideas—including ideas for software products or features—pretty much suck. Even an idea that you absolutely love might offer the customer no value. Worse, it might offer *negative* value.

Most companies decide what products and features to develop without knowing whether their customers even want them. Instead, executives "make decisions based on delusional optimism rather than on a rational weighing of gains, losses, and probabilities," say Dan Lovallo and Daniel Kahneman. They also "overestimate benefits and underestimate costs" and "spin scenarios of success while overlooking the potential for mistakes and miscalculations." So, says, Kahneman, "they pursue initiatives that are unlikely to come in on budget or on time—or to ever deliver the expected returns." Ouch!

Fast customer feedback—customer feedback that's delivered early in the development cycle—is the only way to head off bad ideas before they do too much damage. It can also help companies identify where they can improve their product or feature sooner rather than later. Instead of trying to guess or predict what their customers want, companies find out for sure by obtaining customer feedback.

NOTE

If two customers say they don't like a product or service, that's probably OK. If a million customers say it, then you might have a problem.

How do companies get customer feedback? Here are a few common ways:

- FOCUS GROUPS: This is a small group of people who test a product or feature under development. Companies usually assemble focus groups in person so they can observe their reactions.

- BETA TESTING: This involves sending out a product or feature under development to a select group of users. Beta testing enables companies to uncover flaws in the software before it hits the market.

NOTE

Dogfooding is one type of beta testing. This is when company employees beta test a product or feature themselves. Dogfooding enables companies to identify bugs, glitches, and other problems before their customers do.

- SATISFACTION SURVEYS: These enable companies to gather and measure customer feedback about a product or feature. Although satisfaction surveys are often conducted after a product or feature is released, they could be used earlier in the development process.

- CUSTOMER SUPPORT: A customer service representative's role is to obtain customer feedback. Companies should make sure this feedback loops back to product, development, QA, security, and ops groups.

- SOCIAL MEDIA: Sites like Twitter and Facebook offer a wealth of customer feedback, but this feedback occurs after a product or feature is released.

NOTE

People rarely use social media to praise a product or feature, so most feedback from social media is negative. Negative feedback is still useful, though, as it identifies areas for improvement.

Other ways to obtain customer feedback include building and distributing minimum viable products (MVPs) and conducting A/B testing. For more on these topics, read on.

Minimum Viable Products (MVPs)

A *minimum viable product* (*MVP*) is the simplest, most basic version of a product or feature that still delivers its core functionality. Releasing an MVP is an efficient way to assess the demand for a feature or product early in development.

What About Government Contracts?

Lots of software vendors develop software for government agencies. Obtaining a contract to develop a software product for a government agency generally involves submitting a proposal with a list of suggested features. Like their private sector counterparts, vendors who work for the public sector often generate this list of features with Dan Lovallo and Daniel Kahneman's aforementioned "delusional optimism" and without the "rational weighing of gains, losses, and probabilities."

Of course, the government agency can and usually does provide feedback on this list of features before signing a contract with a vendor. But once the contract is signed, the features are locked in. As a result, a lot of software vendors that work with the government don't worry too much about obtaining customer feedback during the development process.

This might be OK for short-term projects, but for long-term contracts—projects that take many years—it almost certainly isn't. For one thing, it's entirely possible the agency's needs will change. For another, it's just good business to give customers a chance to chime in. Regularly communicating with clients—even a government agency—can result in quality feedback.

An MVP takes much less time to design and build than a full-fledged product or feature, so it enables companies to obtain customer feedback that much faster. Maybe customers will like it and maybe they won't. (Probably they won't.) Either way, the company will know whether they have something good on their hands, and they won't have invested much time, effort, or money to find out if it's worth continuing.

A/B Testing

Companies perform A/B testing by releasing two versions of a product or feature at once. When customers access the product or feature, they are randomly assigned one version or the other. A/B testing enables companies to determine which version their customer prefers. This type of testing is cheap, fast, and informative.

NOTE

A/B testing enables companies to invest minimum time, effort, and money for maximum learning.

What Should Companies Do with Customer Feedback?

The point of customer feedback is to help companies decide whether to do one of three things:

- PIVOT: To pivot is to change direction. When companies pivot, they aren't giving up on the product or feature; they're adapting it based on customer feedback.

- PERSEVERE: To persevere is to stay the course. Companies do this when their customers say their product or feature is a winner.

- STOP: To stop is to abandon development. If customers tell a company that their product or feature doesn't deliver value (or delivers negative value), then the company should stop work immediately, before they sink any more time, effort, or money into it.

The point of *fast* customer feedback is to help companies make that decision as early in the development cycle as possible. To quote the authors of *Lean Enterprise,* "The earlier we can pivot or fold on bad ideas, the less time and resources we waste, and the more we can devote to ideas that will deliver value to our customers—or create new ones."

Conclusion

Obtaining fast feedback is the second key to DevOps. You do this by embedding short feedback loops throughout the value stream.

There are several sources of feedback:

- Automated testing
- Telemetry
- Peers

- Downstream groups

- Customers

Together, these feedback sources help companies ensure they're building the right product or feature and that they're building it in the right way.

The next chapter discusses the third key to DevOps: fostering a positive learning culture.

5

Fostering a Positive Learning Culture

"A positive environment will lead to dramatic benefits for employers, employees and the bottom line."

–Emma Seppälä and Kim Cameron

In This Chapter:
- What Is Organizational Culture?
- Hallmarks of a Positive Learning Culture

The two previous chapters covered the first and second keys of DevOps: maximizing flow and obtaining fast feedback. This chapter is about the third key: fostering a positive learning culture—a culture people actually want to work in.

Maximizing flow and obtaining fast feedback are important. But I'd argue that fostering a positive learning culture is even more so. A company can maximize flow to the nth degree and obtain instantaneous feedback, but if it doesn't build a positive learning culture, then it won't benefit much from DevOps.

Here are just a few of the benefits of a positive learning culture:

- Improved collaboration and teamwork
- Less attrition
- Easier recruitment of top talent

Fostering a positive learning culture also helps to attain Gene Kim's Second and Fourth Ideals: focus, flow, and joy, and psychological safety.

This chapter explains what organizational culture is, covers the types of organizational cultures that lend themselves to DevOps, and offers specific suggestions for fostering a positive learning culture.

What Is Organizational Culture?

Before looking at what constitutes a positive learning culture, it's important to define the term *organizational culture*. This is harder than you might think. There are lots of ways to define organizational culture, but I'm partial to this definition, provided by Shanley Kane in the book *Your Startup Is Broken: Inside the Toxic Culture of Tech Culture*:

> Culture is about power dynamics, unspoken priorities and beliefs, mythologies, conflicts, enforcement of social norms, creation of in/out groups and distribution of wealth and control inside companies.

Pinning down a company's organizational culture is even harder than defining the term. A company's culture is rarely, if ever, articulated. Instead, says Kane, "Our true culture is made primarily of the things no one will say." Emily Freeman agrees, writing that "company culture is best described as the unspoken expectations, behavior, and values of an organization."

Types of Organizational Culture

Sociologist Ron Westrum studied complex aviation and healthcare systems. During his research, Westrum identified three types of organizational cultures:

- PATHOLOGICAL: Organizations with a pathological culture are power-oriented. Higher-ups generally use threats and fear to motivate employees. DevOps cannot thrive in a pathological culture.

- BUREAUCRATIC: Bureaucratic organizations are rules oriented. They do things by the book, although "the book" might vary from group to group. Bureaucratic organizations tend to be highly siloed and allow minimal collaboration. DevOps generally will not succeed in a bureaucratic organization.

- GENERATIVE: A generative organization de-emphasizes hierarchy and promotes collaboration and trust to improve performance. DevOps flourishes in generative organizations.

According to Westrum, whether an organization is pathological, bureaucratic, or generative often dictates how it behaves with respect to cooperation, collaboration, sharing responsibilities, handling information, and failure. (See Table 5.1.)

TABLE 5.1 How Pathological, Bureaucratic, and
Generative Organizations Behave*

Pathological	Bureaucratic	Generative
Cooperation is minimal or non-existent.	Cooperation occurs to a limited degree.	Cooperation is the norm.
Bridge building between teams is opposed.	Bridge building between teams is tolerated but discouraged.	Bridge building between teams is encouraged and rewarded.
Responsibilities are dodged.	Responsibilities are compartmentalized.	Responsibilities (and risks) are shared.
Information is hoarded or concealed.	Information is often disregarded.	Information is sought after.
New ideas are squashed.	New ideas are problematic.	New ideas are sought after and welcomed.
Messengers are shot.	Messengers are tolerated.	Messengers are welcomed and trained.
Failure is covered up or blamed on others.	Failure is met with mercy and justice.	Failure prompts inquiry and learning.

*This table was inspired by a similar one in *Accelerate: The Science of Lean Software and DevOps*, by Nicole Forsgren, Jez Humble, and Gene Kim.

Subsequent studies by other researchers uncovered connections between organization type, performance, and employee burnout. Burnout is as dangerous to our health as second-hand smoke and obesity and can result in a host of mental and emotional symptoms. (Burnout is discussed in more detail later in this chapter.)

A company's size and organizational structure also contribute to its culture. For example, a big company with a hierarchical structure where information flows only from the top down is more likely to be pathological or bureaucratic. In contrast, a small company that gives employees autonomy and encourages open communication is more likely to be generative.

Employee Engagement

Organizational culture is linked to employee engagement. Experts define *employee engagement* as the degree to which an employee is committed to doing their job to the fullest of their ability, and to which the company is committed to ensuring the employee reaches their full potential. As you might guess, pathological and bureaucratic cultures tend to result in lower employee engagement than generative cultures.

Employee engagement is a big deal. Companies with highly engaged employees are more productive and profitable, have higher retention, and report higher customer satisfaction. These days, though, companies with highly engaged employees are rare. According to a 2013 Gallup report, just 30 percent of American workers are engaged; 52 percent are disengaged or tuned out; and 18 percent are *actively* disengaged and undermining everyone else's efforts.

The good news? Fostering a positive learning culture as part of a broader DevOps effort is a sure-fire way to boost employee engagement.

Gauging Organizational Culture

According to psychologist Edgar Schein, you can gauge organizational culture in three main ways:

- BASIC ASSUMPTIONS: People form these over time based on their relationships with others, the way an organization responds to events, and an organization's activities. These assumptions are rarely articulated. They're things people just *know*.

- VALUES: These are an organization's articulated values. Stated goals, strategies, philosophies, and vision statements are examples of values.

- ARTIFACTS: These are observable aspects of an organization's culture—how people dress, what the offices look like, how the company is structured, who tends to be rewarded or fired (and for what), and so on.

NOTE

A company's stated values might be inconsistent with its basic assumptions and artifacts. In such cases, assumptions and artifacts generally offer a better sense of the company's *true* culture.

Hallmarks of a Positive Learning Organizational Culture

You know what organizational culture is and what type is most likely to yield DevOps success. But what does a positive learning culture look like?

Positive learning organizational cultures:

- Offer learning opportunities
- Encourage experimentation
- Accept and learn from failure
- Practice zero blame
- Build trust
- Prevent burnout
- Motivate and reward employees the right way
- Strive to continuously improve

Read on to find out more about each of these practices.

Offering Learning Opportunities

Not to be too obvious, but companies that foster a positive learning culture offer their people lots of opportunities to learn. These could include:

- Traditional classroom training and workshops
- E-learning and web-based training
- Conferences and seminars
- Lunch-and-learns
- Mentoring and coaching
- Pairing

- Stretch assignments
- Task team or committee assignments
- Job rotation and internal transfers
- Self-led study
- Tuition reimbursement

More than that, these companies allocate appropriate funds for learning. This not only ensures that the learning occurs, but it reinforces to employees that the company takes learning seriously.

NOTE

Learning opportunities like these don't only enable employees to pick up new and useful skills. They also help them stay engaged at work.

Encouraging Experimentation

Encouraging experimentation is another hallmark of a positive learning culture. Experimentation involves applying the scientific method to determine which ideas are good ones and which are lemons. This requires the following steps:

1. Developing a hypothesis about a new feature, product, or process
2. Testing whether the hypothesis is true
3. Analyzing the data
4. Drawing conclusions about the feature, product, or process

Experimentation offers other benefits, too, including promoting learning, encouraging employee engagement, and creating a culture in which people actually want to work.

NOTE

Experimentation requires that you accept some level of risk. Otherwise, you'll never get any reward.

One way companies encourage experimentation is by nurturing what Carol S. Dweck calls a *growth mindset* among employees. People with a growth mindset believe they can develop their talents through persistence, hard work, and learning. In other words, "They believe everyone can get smarter if they work at it," say the authors of *Lean Enterprise*. In contrast, people with a fixed mindset think their intelligence, talent, and abilities are traits they cannot change.

> **TIP**
>
> People with personality traits like curiosity, courage, and candor have an easier time adopting a growth mindset. Companies with a positive learning culture tend to hire people with these traits.

Most companies encourage experimentation to quickly test business ideas and to foster innovation and perhaps even disruption. This is critical to success. According to Gene Kim, Kevin Behr, and George Spafford in *The Phoenix Project*, "If you can't out-experiment and beat your competitors in time to market and agility, you are sunk."

Accepting and Learning from Failure

Things go wrong. People make mistakes. Failures happen. Companies with a positive learning culture accept this. Not only do they accept it, they view these failures as learning opportunities.

> **NOTE**
>
> Emily Freeman claims that "failure isn't a marker of stupidity or poor preparation," but is "a marker of growth and a necessary step in innovation."

One way smart, positive companies learn from failure is by holding a special meeting called a *blameless post-mortem* after any failure. In a blameless post-mortem—which should be conducted within three days of the failure at most, and preferably within 36 hours—everyone involved in and affected by the failure gathers to hash over exactly what happened. They then generate a report that describes events, provides a timeline, lists contributing factors, and names possible countermeasures, such as the use of telemetry or automated tests to more quickly detect the conditions that caused the failure.

To provide additional opportunities for learning, some companies even inject faults into their systems. That way, they can learn how to respond to a failure before it occurs in the wild. For example, Netflix developed a tool called Chaos Monkey that randomly kills processes to gauge the system's resilience.

NOTE

Chaos Monkey is just one tool in the so-called Netflix Simian Army. Other tools include Chaos Gorilla, which simulates the failure of an Amazon Web Services (AWS) zone, and Chaos Kong, which replicates the collapse of an entire AWS region.

The Andon Cord

The Toyota Production System (TPS) famously implemented something called the *Andon Cord*. Anytime a worker experienced a problem during production, they pulled this cord. At that point, the whole production line shut down, and everyone stopped what they were doing to swarm the problem until it was solved. That way, the problem didn't snowball and multiply. Immediately solving the problem also ensured that everyone would learn from it.

Many software companies apply a concept like the Andon Cord to their own work. While employees might not pull a physical cord when they experience a problem, they do shut down the pipeline and swarm the problem until they have solved it.

Practicing Zero Blame

One thing that companies with a positive learning organizational culture *don't* do—ever—is cast blame when an experiment goes wrong or some other failure occurs. This practice is called *zero blame*.

Blaming and punishing people when things go wrong makes learning impossible. It also poisons the organizational culture by:

- Causing people to become guarded, keeping problems under wraps until they result in some type of catastrophe

- Fostering fear
- Tanking morale, perhaps resulting in turnover or attrition
- Sowing distrust
- Hindering collaboration

NOTE

Blame and punishment are like poison to organizational culture.

Blame isn't just counterproductive; it's also unfair (another culture killer). Errors that occur in complex processes like those in software development are rarely the fault of any one person. Rather, they are a negative consequence of some aspect of the process itself, such as the steps required or the tools used. Even when a failure is triggered by a specific person, it's rarely that person's fault. It's more likely because the process was not designed to prevent the failure.

Recently I dealt with a manager who publicly blamed an employee for so-called "bad code." The employee's code wasn't perfect, but the appropriate, positive way to address that would have been to speak with the employee in private and to offer positive coaching. By blaming the employee—in public, no less—the manager crushed that person's confidence and morale.

Blame Versus Accountability

Blame is different from accountability. *Blame* is about finding fault. *Accountability*, on the other hand, is when someone accepts responsibility. Put another way, blame is about punishment or even shame, whereas accountability is about ownership.

TIP

Building a zero-blame culture requires a commitment from company leaders (and everyone else) to reward actions that expose problems early on.

Building Trust

Companies with a positive learning culture are characterized by high levels of trust. This trust exists on a team level, among teams, and up and down whatever hierarchy they might have. Indeed, for these companies, trust is the foundation of *all* relationships, personal and professional.

Lack of trust nearly always boils down to an us-versus-them mentality. Indeed, this mentality practically defines the human experience. Sometimes *us* and *them* are members of different tribes or religions. Sometimes they're from different countries. Sometimes they're from the same country but hold opposing political views, live in different neighborhoods, or root for different teams. Sometimes they belong to different social classes or different generations. Sometimes they have different gender or sexual identities. The point is, the us-versus-them mentality is powerful, pervasive, and destructive.

Not surprisingly, such a mentality often exists in the workplace, too. In this context, the dynamic often manifests between different teams or functional roles. It can also arise between management and staff. The latter is especially true when significant inequality exists between these groups—for example, when rank-and-file employees command lower-than-average salaries but company executives are compensated like Gilded Age robber barons and receive special perks like prime parking and private cafeterias.

NOTE

The us-versus-them dynamic is toxic to trust in the workplace—and everywhere else.

Distance often compounds the us-versus-them dynamic at work. I saw this firsthand during a consulting job with a large tech company. I worked primarily with employees at a satellite office near Boulder that handled overflow from the main office in San Diego. The Boulder employees grumbled incessantly about the quality of work from San Diego. Meanwhile, the San Diego employees constantly complained that the Boulder office worked too slowly. Everyone at both offices shared the same goals, though. There was no *them*. There was only *us*. No one seemed to grasp that fact, though, so the negative dynamic persisted, making trust between the two groups impossible.

CAUTION

Outsourcing work overseas often results in a powerful us-versus-them dynamic. Although this is often due in part to language or cultural differences, it usually stems more from a legitimate fear among employees that their roles might be outsourced next. This is one reason some software companies have decided outsourcing overseas just isn't worth it.

How do companies with positive learning cultures defuse an adversarial dynamic to build trust? First and foremost, by encouraging employees to *be nice*. Be kind, look out for others, and support each other. In short, to *not* be jerks. Beyond that, these companies also:

- Facilitate collaboration
- Share responsibilities

The Devopsdays Code of Conduct

Devopsdays is a global series of technical conferences that focus on DevOps practices. The organization behind the series has developed a code of conduct for all Devopsdays events:

- Respect and empathy are core DevOps values. Devopsdays is dedicated to providing an environment where everyone in the DevOps community can learn and share in respectful, considerate collaboration.

- Every devopsdays event has a code of conduct, and we expect the organizer community before, during, and after the conferences to follow a similar code of conduct.

- Devopsdays is dedicated to providing a harassment-free experience for every participant, regardless of gender, sexual orientation, disability, physical appearance, body size, race, religion, or any other personal characteristics. We do not tolerate harassment of anyone in any form. Sexual language and imagery is not appropriate for any devopsdays venue, including Slack, GitHub, and email. Participants violating these rules may be sanctioned or expelled from the organization at the discretion of the core organizers.

- Harassment includes offensive verbal or written comments related to gender, sexual orientation, disability, physical appearance, body size, race, religion, sexual images in public spaces, deliberate intimidation, stalking, following, harassing photography or recording, sustained disruption of talks or other events, inappropriate physical contact, and unwelcome sexual attention. Participants asked to stop any harassing behavior are expected to comply immediately.

Following this code of conduct is one way companies can build trust as part of a broader effort to foster a positive learning culture. For more information about Devopsdays, see https://devopsdays.org.

FACILITATING COLLABORATION

Collaboration is critical to DevOps success in large part because it helps to defuse the us-versus-them mentality. After all, it's hard to think of someone as *other* when they're working right there alongside you in pursuit of the same goal!

Chapter 3, "Maximizing Flow," talked about facilitating collaboration by reorganizing functional groups into small cross-functional teams. Here are a few other ways that companies encourage employees to work together:

- Promote collaboration across teams
- Use collaboration tools (see Appendix B, "Tools for DevOps Success," for more)
- Improve visibility companywide, so everyone can see what everyone else is working on
- Share documentation

SHARING RESPONSIBILITIES

As discussed, teams in so-called normal (non-DevOps) organizations are often siloed. So, responsibilities are siloed, too. The result? You guessed it: an adversarial dynamic—this time between people who own one responsibility and people who own another.

> ## DevOps Is Not a Seating Chart
>
> In recent years, thousands of companies have begun designing their workspaces using an open office concept. In an open office, employees work together in one large room, in full view (and hearing) of each other.
>
> Proponents of open offices say they spur collaboration by encouraging face-to-face communication. This makes them attractive to companies that want to implement DevOps. However, research suggests that open offices actually have the opposite effect. For example, one study shows that people who work in an open office environment have *less* face-to-face communication. One reason is that many workers in open offices wear headphones to drown out the ambient noise, making them less approachable. Another reason is that open offices make private conversations nearly impossible. Perhaps worse, open offices are inherently distracting. They make it harder to complete jobs that require focus and concentration—jobs like writing code.
>
> Open offices aren't all bad. They're cheaper to build and furnish than workspaces with private offices or cubicles, and they look nice. However, companies that choose open offices as a broader DevOps effort are really just rearranging the furniture—nothing more.

This dynamic is made even worse when one group carries out its responsibilities in a way that makes it harder for another group to carry out its responsibilities. A perfect example is when operations teams are charged with responding to all operational incidents, day or night, even though most of those incidents are a result of problematic code written by developers. Operations members often see this as deeply unfair, and rightly so. (To paraphrase *Archer*, "Do you want a revolt? Because that's how you get a revolt.")

The solution in this example is to make it *everyone's* responsibility—developers and operations—to respond to operational incidents. Everyone must be included in the on-call rotation for these events. In addition to defusing the us-versus-them dynamic between operations and development, this practice also:

- Provides developers with immediate feedback when their work results in an operational incident

- Encourages developers to write code with resilience and reliability in mind, which eventually results in fewer operational incidents down the line

- Prevents burnout by distributing the burden of being on call across a larger group

---

NOTE

No one in a positive learning culture *ever* speaks the phrase, "That's not my job."

Companies that are serious about building trust engage in this practice. They also ask employees to share other responsibilities, like:

- Writing documentation
- Conducting tests
- Performing code reviews

Preventing Burnout

Recall from Chapter 1, "Before DevOps," that *burnout* describes a stress-induced physical or mental breakdown. Burnout is dangerous to people's physical, mental, and emotional health, and it can trigger intense symptoms like hopelessness, despair, and even suicide. Needless to say, an organizational culture that causes burnout is *not* a positive one!

Sharing Code, Tooling, and Information

In addition to sharing responsibilities, you can share code, tooling, and information to build trust. This practice has other benefits, too:

- Making everyone's work easier
- Increasing knowledge
- Facilitating collaboration
- Saving time
- Saving money

Burnout has many causes. As discussed in Chapter 1, one cause is work systems that deny employees autonomy and cause them to feel powerless. Here are a few others:

- Excessive work demands
- Inadequate time off
- Insufficient pay
- An unsupportive workplace
- Abrasive co-workers
- A lack of fairness
- A lack of investment in employee development
- No space, time, or resources to experiment and learn
- A lack of purpose
- A difference in values between an individual and the organization

NOTE
Employees who work for pathological organizations are more prone to burnout than employees at generative organizations.

Companies that foster a positive learning environment take concrete steps to head off burnout. Here are a few examples of how they do that:

- Giving employees the autonomy to work in the way that's best for them (more on that in a moment)
- Hiring enough staff to handle work demands
- Honoring a work/life balance
- Instituting humane time-off policies and ensuring that employees take that time
- Refraining from requiring significant overtime
- Paying at least a living wage
- Nurturing a supportive workplace
- Training abrasive employees to improve their behavior (and reprimanding or firing them if they refuse)
- Ensuring fair practices

- Investing in employee development and allowing employees time and space to learn
- Making sure employees are engaged in their work
- Ensuring the organization operates according to its stated values

Motivating and Rewarding Employees the Right Way

Companies cannot foster a positive learning culture if they fail to motivate—and reward—their employees the right way.

Let's talk first about motivation. Psychologists have identified two main types of motivation:

- EXTRINSIC MOTIVATION: When someone is moved to do something by some external reward (such as money, perks, praise, or benefits, for example) or by fear of punishment (including losing a job) for not doing it.

- INTRINSIC MOTIVATION: When someone is driven to do something for its own sake, because it's interesting or satisfying in and of itself.

Extrinsic motivators are important—particularly money—but only to a degree. Everyone needs to be paid *roughly* the industry standard, which should be *at least* a living wage. That prevents employees from spending all their mental energy feeling resentful about not being paid properly and struggling to make ends meet. And of course, no one should be paid less because of gender, gender identity, race, sexuality, physical ability, and the like. However, keep in mind that, according to research, paying people too much can cause them to do *less*. It can also promote undesirable qualities, like greed.

Ultimately, it's *intrinsic* motivators that foster a positive learning culture. These include things like:

- Curiosity
- Challenge
- Autonomy
- Meaning
- Drive
- Purpose
- Camaraderie
- Cooperation

NOTE

When employees work on tasks that tick most or all of these boxes, they are more engaged. They also experience something psychologist Mihaly Csikszentmihalyi calls *flow*. Flow occurs when someone is completely immersed and absorbed in the task at hand, or "in the zone." Flow is one of Gene Kim's Five Ideals.

Autonomy deserves special attention. Employees expect to receive orders from on high about *what* to do. That's fine. But they don't tend to like it so much when higher-ups tell them *how* to do it. When someone tells you what to do and how to do it, taking a *command-and-control* approach, that makes you feel micromanaged, which is a known motivation killer. It also amplifies the us-versus-them dynamic by pitting employees against management. It's far better to take a *mission-control* management style. With mission control, leaders supply employees with a vision, but leave them to complete that mission however they see fit. Allowing employees this level of autonomy energizes and engages them and fosters a sense of pride in their work.

What about rewards? Although rewards are a kind of extrinsic motivator, they have their place in a positive learning culture, because they offer positive reinforcement.

Maslow's Hierarchy of Needs

In 1943 a psychologist named Abraham Maslow theorized that all people have five basic needs that must be met. Maslow presented these needs in pyramid form. He posited that the needs at the base of the pyramid must be met before a person can identify higher-level needs (let alone meet those needs). From the base of the pyramid to its top, these needs are as follows:

- **PHYSIOLOGICAL:** People must have air, food, water, sleep, and shelter.

- **SAFETY:** People must feel safe from physical and mental harm.

- **SOCIAL:** People must have love in their lives and feel a sense of belonging or camaraderie.

- **ESTEEM:** People need to feel respected (by themselves and by others).

- **SELF-ACTUALIZATION:** People need to realize their full potential.

If Maslow's pyramid is correct—and considerable research suggests that it is—it's impossible to foster a positive learning culture if the culture fails to meet these basic human needs.

When most people think of rewards, they think of money—usually salaries and bonuses. However, money is just one type of reward, and it rarely is the best one. Other rewards can include promotions, training and development, time off, or flex time. Companies can also do little things, like hand out gift cards or prizes when employees go above and beyond. And of course, it's always possible to reward someone simply by telling them, privately or publicly, "Hey, great job on that thing you did!"

Communicating the Mission

Too often, software teams find themselves developing and delivering code without really understanding *why.* They know that they're building software, but they don't see the value of their own work or how it fits into their company's broader mission. That prevents them from really engaging. Companies must communicate that broader mission—and do it often. This not only helps people grasp the value of what they're doing day to day, but it also inspires them to take more care in their work.

Striving to Continuously Improve

Chapter 3 discussed the importance of practicing continuous improvement to expedite the flow of work through the value stream. Practicing continuous improvement can help improve a company's culture, too.

Continuous cultural improvement can occur at various levels, including the organizational level, the team level, and the personal level. Of these three, improvement at the personal level often proves most effective, with employees taking initiative and making the changes they want to see at their workplace. For example, if employees want a kinder and more supportive culture, they can be kinder and more supportive themselves. This sets a powerful example! Employees can also improve company culture by acquiring new knowledge, even if it's on their own time and their own dime.

NOTE

Improving culture is the single most important thing a company can do in its effort to implement DevOps.

Conclusion

The third key to DevOps is fostering a positive learning culture. You can describe this type of culture as generative.

A positive learning culture:

- Offers learning opportunities
- Encourages experimentation
- Accepts and learns from failure
- Practices zero blame
- Builds trust
- Prevents burnout
- Motivates and rewards employees the right way
- Continuously strives to improve

The next chapter covers key IT roles in the DevOps model, explains how those roles might differ from their counterparts in more traditional organizations, discusses how best to organize teams in a DevOps environment, and details how to ensure successful teams.

6

DevOps Roles

"It is not the strongest of the species that survive, nor the most intelligent, but the one most responsive to change."

–Charles Darwin

In This Chapter:

- Common DevOps Roles
- Mapping Traditional Roles to DevOps

DevOps has changed the way people build software. So, it's no surprise that some roles in DevOps are new and different, too.

This chapter talks about common DevOps roles and identifies which ones are new, different, or essentially the same.

Common DevOps Roles

DevOps involves many of the same roles as the waterfall model. However, it's often the case that under DevOps, these roles take on different tasks, which might bleed into other functional areas. In addition, a few new roles have evolved to facilitate DevOps.

Common DevOps roles include:

- Product manager
- Enterprise architect
- Systems administrator
- Database administrator
- Software developer
- Cloud engineer
- Security engineer
- Test automation engineer
- Automation engineer
- Site reliability engineer (SRE)
- Subject matter expert (SME)

This section describes each of these DevOps roles in more detail.

NOTE

Having a general understanding of—and a real respect for—each role in a DevOps environment will help you in your quest for DevOps success.

Product Manager

A *product manager* is someone who identifies a need for a product or feature and ushers it from its inception to its release and beyond.

Product management is a business function. However, product managers must collaborate closely with other groups, including those groups responsible for creating, testing, and deploying the product or feature—hence their inclusion in a DevOps environment.

"DevOps Engineer"

Lately, I've noticed that employers have begun placing job advertisements for "DevOps engineers." I contend there's no such thing. To quote Emily Freeman in *DevOps For Dummies*, "DevOps is not a job title. It's a philosophy, a methodology, and an approach to removing friction in the software delivery cycle."

I suspect what these companies are *really* advertising for are software developers or operations engineers (or any number of other roles) who are conversant in the principles and practices of DevOps.

TIP

Learning Agile practices can help product managers interface with more technical types in a DevOps environment.

Enterprise Architect

An *enterprise architect* is someone who bridges the gap between the business function (often represented by the product manager) and the IT function. Essentially, the enterprise architect translates the product or feature put forth by the product manager for IT and develops a concrete plan for its production.

According to Sharon Florentine of *CIO* magazine, the role of enterprise architect "requires a combination of skills, from network administration to cloud to traditional systems administrator capabilities." Florentine continues: "In addition, someone in an enterprise architect role should be proficient in systems thinking, strategic thinking, project management, IT governance and operations" and have "extensive hardware and software knowledge."

Systems Administrator

A *systems administrator* is responsible for the smooth operation of the computer and network systems used in the course of daily business (including for software development). These systems can be very complicated.

The role of a systems administrator in a DevOps shop isn't markedly different from the role in a waterfall environment, except systems administrators might take on tasks that relate to using virtual environments or other cloud tools.

Some systems administrators who work in DevOps might opt to change to one of two different roles: site reliability engineer (SRE) or subject matter expert (SME). You'll learn more about each of these roles later in this chapter.

Database Administrator

A *database administrator* creates, maintains, backs up, queries, tunes, and secures databases throughout the company, including those used for the purposes of software development.

In more traditional environments, database engineers tend to work primarily with systems administrators and operations engineers. In DevOps, however, they collaborate more closely with the development team to design the data stores and communications to and from databases to ensure higher performance and heightened security.

TIP

Database administrators in DevOps can learn programming and scripting languages beyond SQL to become even more relevant.

Software Developer

A *software developer* writes the source code that serves as the foundation of a digital product, service, or feature. Software developers have deep knowledge of at least one computer language (for example, C++ or Java).

Under the waterfall model, software developers focused almost entirely on writing code. With DevOps, however, they might take on additional tasks. For example:

- Provisioning their own environments
- Testing their code to ensure quality and security
- Deploying their code to production

- Troubleshooting problems with their code
- Supporting their code after deployment

Cloud Engineer

A *cloud engineer* is someone who designs, plans, manages, maintains, and supports technology associated with the cloud—for example, virtual machines used to provision programming environments or host applications. Many DevOps practices are made easier by the cloud!

NOTE

Think of a cloud engineer as a systems engineer who specializes in cloud technologies.

Security Engineer

With waterfall, the role of the *security engineer* is to test code to ensure that it is secure—that is, free of bugs, holes, and other vulnerabilities. These tests are manual, meaning they consume a lot of time. And they're run late in the development cycle, so it's time-consuming and costly to fix any problems they uncover—sometimes so much so that companies are forced to ship the flawed software as is.

With DevOps, things are different. Under DevOps, most security tests can be or should be automated. They can also be run earlier in the development cycle. This frees the security engineer to:

- Help design the application with privacy and security in mind
- Coach developers on avoiding common vulnerabilities
- Guide developers to make sure code is written with test automation in mind
- Provide tools to developers to improve security, such as shared source code repositories and libraries
- Develop and perform automated security tests to expedite security checks and ensure regulatory compliance
- Build telemetry to identify security problems

In other words, as the authors of *Accelerate: The Science of DevOps* say, "What we see here is a shift from information security teams doing the security reviews themselves to giving developers the means to build security in." Security becomes part of *everyone's* job.

NOTE

Providing feedback from security (and other functions) earlier in the development cycle is called *shifting left*. For more on shifting left, refer to Chapter 3, "Maximizing Flow."

DevSecOps

Some people use the term *DevSecOps* to describe the practice of shifting security tasks left. I think it's overkill. Because DevOps practices already call for a leftward shift, that feels redundant. Despite that, lots of security types like the term.

Test Automation Engineer

Some waterfall shops employ what they call *test engineers*. The precise role of a test engineer differs from company to company. For example, in some companies, the test engineer role pertains primarily to quality assurance—in other words, ensuring code meets all quality and regulatory standards. In other companies, however, the role has a broader scope. Regardless, most test engineers have one thing in common: They focus on performing manual tests.

In a waterfall environment, manual tests for quality assurance or anything else result in the same problems as manual security tests. That is, they take up a lot of time and they're performed late in the development cycle—well after any issues they reveal can be quickly, cheaply, and easily fixed.

DevOps solves these problems by adapting the test engineer role into something new: test automation engineer. Test automation engineers devote their efforts to designing new automated tests. This approach frees them to focus on many of the same tasks as security engineers: helping developers design the application with test automation and quality in mind, coaching developers on avoiding common quality problems, and so on.

Automation Engineer

DevOps calls for the automation of as many rote and repetitive tasks as possible—things like provisioning the development, generating builds, staging, packaging, deploying, releasing, reporting, and more. An *automation engineer*, then, identifies tasks that can be automated, and designs, implements, and monitors automation processes to handle those tasks.

NOTE

Automation engineer is a relatively new role. Originally, the tasks associated with this role were completed on an *ad hoc* basis. As more and more companies have adopted DevOps, the role has become formalized.

In some DevOps environments, the role of automation engineer has replaced a different role: release engineer. A *release engineer* ensures that all hardware and software components in a product or feature work together as they should. This involves building and overseeing the release platform, assessing software performance, and setting the release schedule. Many of these tasks are automated under DevOps.

The Path Forward for Release Engineers

If you're a release engineer and you want to work in DevOps, you might consider transitioning to the automation engineer role. Alternatively, if as a release engineer you focused more on processes and rules than on technical practices, you might become what's called a scrum master. *Scrum* is an Agile methodology that enables teams to self-organize and work quickly in accordance with Agile principles. A *scrum master* manages the process of exchanging information.

Automation engineers also take over many tasks associated with configuration management (CM) engineers. This means CM engineers must shift their focus to enhancing the value stream by eliminating unneeded gates and low-value constraints (or to becoming automation engineers themselves).

Am I Automating Myself Out of a Job?

Some people worry that DevOps' emphasis on automation will result in fewer jobs. In my view, this worry is unfounded. In my experience, automating rote and repetitive processes simply frees engineers to focus on more challenging, interesting, and important tasks. In other words, under DevOps, there are still plenty of jobs to do; they're just *different* jobs.

Site Reliability Engineer (SRE)

A *site reliability engineer* (*SRE*) is someone who applies aspects of software engineering to solve problems associated with infrastructure and operations. The SRE's main goal is to create systems that are scalable and highly reliable.

The SRE role in DevOps maps to a different role in more traditional environments: operations engineer. An *operations engineer* ensures that all end user–facing systems are up and running. Operations engineers also supply developers with programming environments and deploy and maintain code. As noted, DevOps calls for developers to take up these tasks, hence the evolution of the SRE role in a DevOps environment.

Some SREs might be better described as *full-stack engineers*. A full-stack engineer is someone who has a basic grasp of every step in the software development process and all associated technologies.

Subject Matter Expert (SME)

A subject matter expert (SME) is someone who has special skills or knowledge in a specific area, such as a particular tool, cloud provider, or methodology. Often, SMEs have deep domain knowledge of your product or of your customer's requirements.

Mapping Traditional Roles to DevOps

Again, some traditional IT roles have evolved under DevOps. Table 6.1 shows which roles have changed, and which have remained the same (although the roles might involve some different tasks). If you work in a more traditional role, this table can help you find a path forward within DevOps.

TABLE 6.1   Traditional Roles Mapped to DevOps Roles

Traditional Role	DevOps Role
Product manager	Product manager
Enterprise architect	Enterprise architect
Systems administrator	Systems administrator Site reliability engineer (SRE) Subject matter expert (SME) Cloud engineer
Database administrator	Database administrator
Software developer	Software developer
Security engineer	Security engineer
Release engineer	Automation engineer Scrum master
Test engineer	Test automation engineer
Configuration management engineer	Automation engineer
Operations engineer	Site reliability engineer Full-stack engineer

---

DevOps Versus No Ops

Many interpret DevOps to mean no ops—in other words, the complete elimination of the operations function. This is not the case. While it's true that the nature of operations work does shift with DevOps—from performing manual work to deploy products or features to providing APIs, self-service platforms, and other tools to facilitate development work—the operations group remains as important as ever.

This is important, so let me repeat it: *With DevOps, the operations group remains as important as ever.*

The most successful teams consist of people with solid development skills *and* solid ops skills working together.

Conclusion

DevOps means using different practices and tools to develop software. That also means changing certain roles in the software development process.

This chapter discussed the various roles involved in DevOps and noted if and how they differ from those in a traditional approach:

- Product manager
- Enterprise architect
- Systems administrator
- Database administrator
- Software developer
- Cloud engineer
- Security engineer
- Test automation engineer
- Automation engineer
- Site reliability engineer (SRE)
- Subject matter expert (SME)

The next chapter talks about positioning yourself for a career in DevOps.

7
Positioning Yourself for a Career in DevOps

"Those that adopt DevOps will win in the marketplace,
at the expense of those that do not."

–Gene Kim, Jez Humble,
Patrick Debois, and John Willis

In This Chapter:

- Critical Skills and Knowledge
- Training and Education
- Personal Qualities, Behaviors, and Attitudes

Maybe your company has announced plans to adopt DevOps, and you need to figure out how to adapt. Perhaps you want to implement DevOps practices in your own work (and convince everyone else to do so, too). Or maybe you keep hearing how great DevOps is, and you want to make yourself more marketable to companies that use it.

This chapter covers the critical skills and knowledge you need to thrive in a DevOps environment. It also discusses training and education you can pursue to obtain these skills and knowledge. Finally, it spells out personal qualities, behaviors, and attitudes that can help you succeed in DevOps.

Critical Skills and Knowledge

To quote DevOps expert Patrick Debois, when it comes to DevOps, "there is no one IT skill that is more useful or more powerful than another." Instead, DevOps calls for people who have a variety of skills and knowledge.

Of course, some of these elements will be technical. You needn't have expertise in all these areas, but a working knowledge is helpful:

- THE SOFTWARE DEVELOPMENT LIFE CYCLE: A basic understanding of the steps required to design, develop, and deploy software is critical. Even better: the ability to perform different tasks throughout the life cycle.

- THE VALUE CHAIN: Knowing the general steps needed to build a particular product is critical.

- DATABASES: These could include both SQL and NoSQL databases.

- SERVERS: These could include servers for components like web, applications, clients, proxies, and so on.

- PROGRAMMING LANGUAGES: Useful programming languages include Java, Groovy, C++, C#, and Go.

- SCRIPTING LANGUAGES: Knowledge in scripting languages like Bash, Python, Perl, and Ruby is helpful.

- SECURITY: A working knowledge of security principles, practices, and tools is important.

- CONTINUOUS INTEGRATION, DELIVERY, AND DEPLOYMENT: Continuous integration means continually committing small batches of code; continuous delivery involves keeping code in a continuously deployable state; and continuous deployment means constantly deploying code to an operations (or operations-like) environment.

- THE DEPLOYMENT PIPELINE: This includes automated environment provisioning and security and quality testing, continuous integration, version control, and automated deployment.

- AUTOMATION: A basic understanding of how automation works and what you can use it for (hint: lots of stuff) is helpful.

- TOOLS: Many tools facilitate DevOps. For information about specific tools, see Appendix B, "Tools for DevOps Success."

Other critical skills and knowledge are the "soft" variety, like communication and collaboration skills.

TIP

Recall from Chapter 3, "Maximizing Flow," that teams should be organized in a T formation, with deep expertise in one area and more cursory knowledge in others. It's a good idea for people to follow a similar pattern, becoming extremely fluent in one technical topic and at least conversant in others.

Communication Skills

Early in my career, I worked on a team with a dozen or so software engineers for a company that created video-conferencing systems. I was the release engineer, and my job was to integrate their code into each new product build for deployment. Releasing a new build generally involved me pulling an all-nighter on Friday to compile the code and deploying it early Saturday morning.

After one of these all-nighters, when I'd gone home to rest, the test engineers flagged a problem: a key new feature was missing. I was called back into the office. When I arrived, a gaggle of managers attacked me.

"Where's the new feature?" one of them demanded.

"I don't know," I said, flustered. I quickly verified that I had merged all the requested changes. "I merged all the code I was given. I don't know what happened to it!"

Things went downhill from there. "What do you mean you don't know what happened to it?" they cried. "How could you lose it?" "It's a critical feature!" "How stupid can you be?" They even got the vice president on the phone to pile on.

Finally, after what seemed like an eternity, one of the lead software engineers wandered by. "Hey," he said. "What's going on?"

"The new build is missing a key feature!" one of the managers yelled.

The software engineer reached into his shirt pocket, pulled out a disk, and set it on my desk. "I don't know why you're yelling at Shawn," he said. "The code is right here."

I tell this story to my clients all the time because it illustrates so many different bad behaviors. But ultimately, this story is about poor communication—by the software engineer *and* the managers.

It's impossible to overstate the importance of good communication in software development. Everyone who works in the software development value stream must communicate effectively with everyone else. This is true in any organization, whether it employs DevOps or not!

You can communicate in many ways: face to face, phone, e-mail, text, IM, and more. Different methods offer different advantages. For example, communicating over e-mail, text, or IM is quick and easy, and results in a written record of the exchange. These methods are good for purely informative exchanges. (Phone calls work well for these types of exchanges, too.) But they might not be appropriate for more complex or emotional conversations. For those, face-to-face conversations are best.

TIP

Face-to-face conversations are the *only* way to deliver bad news or resolve conflicts.

Often, it's not so much what you say but how you say it. That's where more complex communication skills come in. Here are a few examples:

- When communicating face to face, look the person you're talking to in the eye and pay attention to your tone of voice and body language.
- Listen more than you talk. (Try for 80 percent listening and 20 percent talking.) And listen *actively*. Don't judge what they are saying and don't form rebuttals while they are speaking.
- When someone else finishes speaking, paraphrase what they said to ensure you heard them correctly.
- When speaking face to face or on the phone, direct all your attention to the conversation. Don't multitask. Only take phone calls when you have time (and are willing) to talk.
- If you miss a call, return it promptly.
- Don't send messages when your emotions are running high. It's all too easy to send a scathing missive when you're mad. Don't do it!

- Use descriptive subject headings with email and keep messages brief.

- In all forms of written communication—texts and IMs included —use proper grammar, punctuation, capitalization, and spelling. DON'T USE ALL CAPS.

- *Never* write or say anything that could be interpreted as libelous, racist, sexist, homophobic, anti-Semitic, or xenophobic—even if you think you are being funny.

NOTE

People from different cultures may communicate differently. You should be aware of these differences when communicating with others.

Nonverbal Communication

When most people think of communication, they think of speaking and listening, or *verbal communication*. But there's another more subtle type of communication: nonverbal communication.

Body language, the most common form of nonverbal communication, includes gestures, posture, and facial expressions. Other forms include physical appearance and *proxemics* (physical distance between people).

Research suggests that nonverbal communication accounts for more than 65 percent of all messages received during an exchange. So, in addition to improving your verbal communication skills, you need to cultivate your nonverbal ones, too. Here are a few tips:

- RELAX: If you stay relaxed, chances are everyone else will, too.

- BE SELF-AWARE: Notice when your body language is negative —for example, if you're pointing, shrugging, slouching, or rolling your eyes. Then knock it off.

- GO EASY ON THE GESTURES: If you use certain gestures too often, they can lose their effectiveness.

NOTE

Not everyone is a natural-born communicator. Fortunately, communication skills can be learned!

Collaboration Skills

If you've read this far, you've probably already grasped the importance of collaboration in a DevOps environment. So, it follows that having solid collaboration skills and demonstrating positive collaborative behaviors are critical. Table 7.1 lists several examples.

TABLE 7.1 Collaboration Skills and Collaborative Behaviors*

Communication Skills	Interpersonal Skills	Emotional Intelligence
Respect for diversity	Building consensus	Assessing the strengths and weaknesses of others
Delegating	Solving problems	Identifying obstacles to success
Mediating conflict	Compromising	Not blaming
Accepting constructive criticism	Analytical skills	Thinking critically
Brainstorming	Demonstrating creativity	Demonstrating emotional stability
Showing diligence	Showing reliability	Showing humor
Time-management skills	Deadline-management skills	Resource-management skills

*This table is adapted from "Collaboration Skills: Definition, List, and Examples" by Alison Doyle (see http://www.thebalancecareers.com/collaboration-skills-with-examples-2059686)

In addition to honing your collaboration skills and collaborative behaviors to adapt to a DevOps environment, it might also be helpful to learn your way around various tools designed to facilitate collaboration. These might include general collaboration tools like:

- Microsoft Office Suite
- Skype

- GoToMeeting
- Zoom
- Google Docs
- Slack

They might also include tools designed specifically to support collaboration during the software development process. Appendix B, "Tools for DevOps Success," lists several of these tools.

Good communication is particularly important when dealing with conflict. This involves skills and behaviors like:

- Actively listening
- Paying attention to nonverbal communication
- Remaining calm
- Using humor to defuse the situation and lighten the mood (assuming the conflict is not of a sensitive nature)
- Keeping an open mind
- Being curious about how the other person arrived at their position
- Showing empathy and compassion for the other person's position
- Assuming goodwill on the other person's part
- Avoiding being defensive or easily offended
- Avoiding an accusatory tone
- Focusing only on the current conflict (not rehashing old conflicts)
- Searching for and suggesting reasonable solutions
- Identifying and resolving systemic problems that may have contributed to the conflict
- Showing a willingness to compromise
- Not blaming
- Knowing when to apologize and when to forgive

TIP

Be proactive. Don't let a situation spiral out of control simply because you failed to communicate.

Collaborating with Difficult People

Collaboration isn't always easy—especially when it involves working with difficult people. Keep these tips in mind when you are collaborating with someone who's just plain hard to deal with:

- RECOGNIZE THEIR EXPERTISE: Sometimes difficult people just want a little credit.

- SEEK THEIR HELP: Some difficult people are difficult because they believe they have more to offer than they've been asked to contribute. Ask them.

- STAY FOCUSED: Difficult people are notorious complainers— often about problems that are outside their control or that can never be fixed. Don't allow yourself to be pulled into conversations about these topics.

- SET YOUR BOUNDARIES: Difficult people often like to see how far they can push others. Make it clear from the start where your boundaries lie.

- DON'T TAKE THE BAIT: If a difficult person tosses a verbal grenade your way, it's far better to dodge it than to catch it or toss it back.

NOTE

Ultimately, collaboration eliminates the us-versus-them dynamic that is so toxic to organizations. This makes good collaboration skills invaluable!

Training and Education

Working in a DevOps environment doesn't take special training or education beyond the computer science degrees generally required for any IT job. However, loads of resources are available to get you up to speed on DevOps principles and practices. Appendix A, "DevOps Resources," lists several specific DevOps-related resources, including books, websites, blogs, podcasts, online courses, webinars, conferences, and more.

TIP

Don't wait for your employer to offer training. Go out and get it!

DevOps Certification

At present, there is no such thing as DevOps certification. However, it *is* possible to become certified in many DevOps-related tools. Is obtaining certification for DevOps tools absolutely necessary? Probably not. But it doesn't hurt, especially if you don't have a lot of on-the-job experience. Appendix A contains links to information about several DevOps-related certifications.

Personal Qualities, Behaviors, and Attitudes

Earlier chapters in this book discussed how culture is *the* most important aspect of DevOps. Maximizing flow and obtaining instantaneous feedback are great, but without a positive learning culture, DevOps simply isn't doable.

As mentioned, a company's culture is made up of many things: power dynamics, priorities, beliefs, mythologies, conflicts, norms, in groups and out groups, the distribution of wealth and control, and so on. But that's not all. A company's culture is also a reflection of the personal qualities, attitudes, and behaviors of everyone who works there.

It follows, then, that one way to develop a positive culture—one that allows for successful DevOps implementation—is to adopt positive personal qualities, attitudes, and behaviors. Like John Shook, who helped implement TPS during the 1980s at an automotive plant in California, says: "The way to change culture is not to first change how people think, but instead to start by changing how people behave—what they do."

You can adopt several personal qualities, attitudes, and behaviors to improve your chances of succeeding in a DevOps environment. Here are just a few:

- BE A TEAM PLAYER: DevOps is all about teamwork. Cowboy types who like to go it alone generally do not thrive in a DevOps environment. Neither do glory seekers. This is true even if they are excellent at performing the technical tasks associated with their job. You and your team are in it together, so everyone needs to act like it.

- MAKE FRIENDS UP AND DOWN THE VALUE STREAM: Don't limit your circle to other people on your team or in your functional group. Build relationships with people up and down the value stream.

- **PLAY DOWN POLITICS:** Don't cause or become embroiled in political upheaval at work. Remember: Everyone is on the same side!

- **BE NICE:** Building trust is key to any successful DevOps effort, but building trust with people who aren't nice is pretty much impossible. Unkind or confrontational people tend to inflame the toxic us-versus-them dynamic. They also tend to provoke fear in others.

- **BE INCLUSIVE:** Make a special effort to look out for co-workers who are members of marginalized groups.

- **HAVE EMPATHY:** Other people's jobs are hard. Other people's *lives* are hard. Don't forget that.

- **ASSUME THE BEST OF OTHERS:** If you have a conflict with another person or group, give them the benefit of the doubt. Most people don't make it their mission to inflict misery upon you, specifically.

- **IMPROVE YOURSELF:** Just as DevOps involves applying continuous improvement to products and processes, it also means applying it to people—including you. Continuously strive to improve your knowledge, your skills, and your manner.

- **BE CURIOUS:** Be curious about people. Be curious about their work. Be curious about *your* work. Then act on that curiosity.

- **KEEP LEARNING:** Don't become complacent in your knowledge. When you work in IT, everything changes, all the time. Not a week goes by that I don't find out about a new tool or technology! Keep up with these changes and think about how you can apply them to your own work.

TIP

Not all your training and education must be formal. Simply staying abreast of new developments in DevOps counts.

- **EMBRACE CHANGE:** Change will happen. Don't fight it. Figure out how to make it work for you. Show flexibility and adapt as conditions change.

- **SHOW INITIATIVE:** Do you notice something that needs doing? Then do it. Don't wait around for someone else to tell you to. (Just be sure you avoid veering into cowboy behavior.)

- WORK HARD: Implementing DevOps is hard work. The good news? Once DevOps is in place, it can do wonders to ease your workload, freeing you to focus on the stuff that really matters and that you're really good at.

- KEEP AN OPEN MIND: Don't become entrenched in one way of thinking about products, processes, or people.

- CONSIDER THE BIG PICTURE: Bridge the gap between your own expertise and the broader challenges facing your company.

Conclusion

This chapter outlines the critical skills and knowledge you need to shift to a DevOps environment, to promote its adoption, and to make yourself more marketable to DevOps companies. It also suggests training and education to help you transition to DevOps. Finally, it describes the personal qualities, behaviors, and attitudes that can help you adapt to DevOps.

The next chapter presents pitfalls to avoid in a DevOps effort.

8

Steering Clear of Common Pitfalls

*"Nothing in the world is worth having or worth doing
unless it means effort, pain, difficulty."*

–Theodore Roosevelt

In This Chapter:

- Plan Your DevOps Initiative
- Get Leadership Buy-In
- Go All In
- Don't Scrimp on Resources
- Don't Just Pay Lip Service
- Model DevOps to Fit Your Needs
- Prioritize Culture
- Stamp Out the Us-Versus-Them Mentality
- Choose People Carefully
- Don't Demand Heroics

Switching to DevOps isn't easy. It takes hard work and commitment. There will be obstacles along the way. This chapter points to some pitfalls that are common in a DevOps effort and offers practical advice to help companies avoid them.

Plan Your DevOps Initiative

Nobody likes change. And with good reason! Even positive change pushes people outside their comfort zone. When companies decide to transition to DevOps, they must take special care to manage that change. Otherwise, everyone will freak out.

First and foremost, managing the transition requires communication, and lots of it. Specifically, company leaders must communicate why they want to implement DevOps, how they plan to do so, how long they think it will take, and what benefits it will bring. Otherwise, employees will draw their own conclusions about the effort, and those conclusions will almost certainly be negative.

Company leaders should also:

- SOLICIT FEEDBACK: Employees will have concerns about changing to DevOps. Urge employees to voice these concerns and address them as transparently as your business allows. Also ask employees to share any suggestions they might have for smoothing the transition.

- GET BUY-IN: The more people buy into the DevOps program, the more successful it will be. Communicating is one way to get buy-in. So is soliciting feedback.

- TAKE IT SLOWLY: Don't move too quickly. Make incremental changes. Otherwise, you risk leaving people behind. Be patient; it might be weeks or even months before DevOps initiatives bear fruit.

- OFFER TRAINING: As you saw in Chapter 6, "DevOps Roles," the tasks associated with various jobs may change under DevOps. Companies must make sure everyone has the training they need to take on these new tasks.

- GIVE POSITIVE REINFORCEMENT: Because change pushes people outside their comfort zone, they often feel vulnerable during change events. It's important to make them feel appreciated by rewarding positive behaviors and celebrating accomplishments whenever you can. (That said, avoid relying on metrics to reward employees. Otherwise, people will just find ways to game the system.)

NOTE

Communicating during transitions means passing information down the chain *and* up it.

Company leaders aren't the only ones who can affect the success of a DevOps initiative. Employees can, too. Here are some tips for employees transitioning to a DevOps environment:

- ASK QUESTIONS: If you're not clear on some aspect of the transition, don't fill in the blanks. Instead, get the facts from someone who knows.

- CONCENTRATE ON YOUR WORK: Don't get caught up in the whirlwind. Focus on your tasks.

- LEVERAGE THE CHANGE TO YOUR ADVANTAGE: Identify ways to use and improve your skills, knowledge, and abilities in the new environment.

- ASK FOR HELP: Speak up about how the company, your manager, and your co-workers can support you during the transition.

Get Leadership Buy-In

Leadership buy-in is critical to any DevOps effort. Without it, the effort may not succeed. Make sure company leaders are on board.

Your DevOps effort will have an even better chance of success if company leaders practice *transformational leadership*. According to the authors of *Accelerate*, this describes a leadership style that is characterized by:

- VISION: Leaders have a clear view of where the company is going and how it will get there.

- INTELLECTUAL STIMULATION: Leaders push others to ponder problems and processes in new and creative ways.

- INSPIRATIONAL COMMUNICATION: Leaders motivate others by appealing to their values and sense of purpose.

- SUPPORTIVE LEADERSHIP: Leaders demonstrate care, consideration, and compassion for others.

- PERSONAL RECOGNITION: Leaders notice, acknowledge, praise, and reward other people's outstanding efforts.

By the way, leaders who practice transformational leadership also help:

- Establish a positive learning culture (read more in Chapter 5, "Fostering a Positive Learning Culture")
- Facilitate communication and collaboration company-wide
- Bridge or even eliminate silos
- Promote experimentation and innovation
- Improve performance
- Reduce turnover

Go All In

Often, companies implement only a few aspects of DevOps. They buy a couple of tools, or they change a few processes. Then, when they don't see the gains they were hoping for, they give up.

Don't do this. If you're going to adopt DevOps, go all in. That means implementing as many DevOps principles, practices, and tools as you can, such as:

- Establishing small cross-functional teams
- Eliminating waste and bottlenecks
- Making work visible and prioritizing important work
- Practicing continuous integration, deployment, and delivery
- Building a deployment pipeline with automated testing and version control
- Automating routine tasks
- Using cloud technologies
- Creating short feedback loops
- Using telemetry
- Obtaining customer feedback
- Cultivating a positive learning culture

NOTE

A successful DevOps effort requires adopting all three of its key approaches: maximizing flow, obtaining fast feedback, and fostering a positive learning culture.

Don't Scrimp on Resources

DevOps doesn't just happen. Implementing and sustaining DevOps takes time and resources. Failing to allocate appropriate resources will doom a DevOps effort. Companies must provide the people, processes, and tools needed to do it right.

NOTE

Of course, exactly how many people, processes, and tools are necessary, and what type, will vary from company to company.

That's not all, though. Companies must also allocate appropriate resources to building a positive learning environment—somewhere people actually want to work. Does this mean remodeling the office and furnishing it with ping-pong tables and massage chairs? No. It means committing the resources needed to foster learning, prevent burnout, and motivate employees.

Don't Just Pay Lip Service

A few years back, I noticed that steampunk had become popular. What started as an obscure subgenre of science fiction that reimagined Victorian England as a technologically advanced society but with clunky wood and metal steam-powered gadgets had morphed into a design aesthetic. Pretty soon, it seemed like everyone was gluing metal gears onto modern products and calling them *steampunk*. Of course, these products aren't *really* steampunk, because they don't add meaningful function, just aesthetics.

Sometimes I feel like the same thing happens with technological transitions like the one to DevOps. Companies glue a few gears onto their old systems and processes and say they're doing DevOps. It isn't enough to just *say* you're doing DevOps, though. If you want to reap the benefits, you have to actually *do* DevOps. That means adopting DevOps practices, tools, and behaviors to maximize flow, obtain fast feedback, and foster a positive learning environment.

On a related note, some organizations try to limit their DevOps program to a single team, which they call the *DevOps team*. This is also just paying lip service. Creating a team but failing to adopt the practices across the board is simply creating a new silo and *saying* you're doing DevOps.

Model DevOps to Fit Your Needs

There's no one blueprint for doing DevOps. Different companies implement DevOps in different ways. What works for one company might not work for another, meaning that simply copying some other company's playbook won't fly.

Your DevOps effort must be just that: *your* DevOps effort. Tailor it to your organization and teams. That doesn't mean you shouldn't study and learn from how other companies implement DevOps. It just means you shouldn't assume that what works for them will work for you.

NOTE

There's no prescription or one right way. Companies must tailor their DevOps efforts to suit their own needs.

Prioritize Culture

A company could spend a trillion dollars on tools and consultants to maximize flow and obtain instantaneous feedback, but if company culture isn't prioritized, their DevOps efforts will fail.

This probably sounds strange from a person who has built a consulting company around tools, but I see it all the time. Some clients invest thousands of dollars on tools and services but deprioritize the cultural component, and are surprised when their efforts fizzle out.

I get why this happens. Tools are straightforward. You buy them, you use them, and you see results. Culture is trickier. It's more complex and much harder to change. But change it you must. A successful switch to DevOps calls for a complete commitment to the cultivation of a positive company culture.

NOTE

Chapter 5, "Fostering a Positive Learning Culture," has lots of information on cultivating this kind of culture.

Stamp Out the Us-Versus-Them Mentality

When a company's DevOps effort flounders, it's almost always because of an us-versus-them mentality. Sometimes this mentality manifests among teams or functional roles, or between management and staff. It can also manifest in other ways:

- Employees who prefer different programming languages
- Employees who like to use different tools
- Employees who take different approaches to completing a task
- Employees who have different personality types
- Employees who prefer different communication methods
- Employees who work different shifts
- Employees who work on-site and those who work from home
- Employees who are from different regions
- Employees who are from different generations
- Employees who have kids and those who don't

I could go on and on. Take special care to avoid inciting an us-versus-them dynamic, detect when such a dynamic exists, and take any steps necessary to defuse it.

Choose People Carefully

Most companies hire new employees based solely on their technical skill set. For example, they may need someone who knows Java and therefore hire someone who knows the language.

Obviously, these types of technical skills are important, but a DevOps environment requires people with other types of skills and personal qualities, too:

- Communication skills
- Collaboration skills
- Leadership skills
- Curiosity
- An ability to quickly process new information on the fly
- An ability to learn from failure
- An ability to mesh with existing staff
- Minimal ego
- Enthusiasm
- Resilience
- Kindness
- Empathy

Of course, people with *all* these qualities are as rare as a Rembrandt, but they are out there. That being said, you'll probably need to step up your recruiting efforts to attract them!

CAUTION

Avoid engineers (or anyone) who think they're the smartest people in the room, refuse to listen to others' ideas, and cannot admit when they're wrong. These types will "silence their colleagues and steamroll anyone who disagrees with them," says Emily Freeman.

Don't Demand Heroics

You're probably familiar with companies that regularly rely on their employees to engage in heroics, working day and night to complete a critical task (or even just to stay on top of their daily work). Maybe you work for such a company.

Calling for constant heroics is a sure-fire way to doom a DevOps effort. It's just not what the model is about. Indeed, one reason DevOps emphasizes practices like teamwork and continuous improvement is that they make heroic efforts unnecessary.

Does this mean heroics are *never* necessary with DevOps? Well, no. Disasters happen, and someone (you) has to step in to save the day. When that happens, you don't want to shy away from it. But you shouldn't be asked to do it every day!

Conclusion

DevOps is hard work. It takes planning and commitment. Committing to the best practices discussed in this chapter can help ensure your efforts aren't in vain.

Committing to learning more is another way to help ensure success. Appendix A, "DevOps Resources," can show you where to start.

Conclusion

Remember Carl? He was the systems administrator I mentioned in the introduction who asked me to help him prepare for his company's transition to DevOps. Carl was worried he'd be left behind—that by taking this new direction, the company would no longer have a spot for him. It was my conversation with Carl—and with others like him, who have sought my advice in their own DevOps journeys—that inspired me to write this book.

You're probably wondering what happened to Carl. Did he successfully navigate his company's transition to DevOps? Well, the last time we spoke, he was much more positive then he had been at our dinner a few years before. He told me he had become an avid podcast listener and had started online courses to improve his programming skills. He had also applied to become an automation engineer inside his company and was expecting to take on that role soon.

By preparing for the transition—educating himself on what DevOps is; its basic principles, practices, and tools; and how it might change his role—Carl positioned himself for DevOps success. The same is true of you. By reading this book, you've set yourself up to thrive under DevOps.

Whether you already work in a DevOps environment, want to move to one, or want to build one yourself, you have the information you need to succeed (and the resources to learn even more).

Best of luck to you in your DevOps journey!

–Shawn D. Doyle

APPENDIX # DevOps Resources

Books

- *Accelerate: The Science of Lean Software and DevOps* by Nicole Forsgren, Jez Humble, and Gene Kim (2018: IT Revolution Press)

- *Continuous Delivery: Reliable Software Releases Through Build, Test, and Deployment Automation* by Jez Humble and David Farley (2011: Addison-Wesley Professional)

- *DevOps For Dummies* by Emily Freeman (2019: John Wiley & Sons)

- *The DevOps Handbook: How to Create World-Class Agility, Reliability, and Security in Technology Organizations* by Gene Kim, Jez Humble, Patrick Debois, and John Willis (2016: IT Revolution Press)

- *Effective DevOps: Building a Culture of Collaboration, Affinity, and Tooling at Scale* by Jennifer Davis and Ryn Daniels (2016: O'Reilly Media)

- *The Goal: A Process of Ongoing Improvement* by Eliyahu M. Goldratt (1984: North River Press)

- *Lean Enterprise: How High Performance Organizations Innovate at Scale* by Jez Humble, Joanne Molesky, and Barry O'Reilly (2015: O'Reilly Media)

- *The Phoenix Project: A Novel About IT, DevOps, and Helping Your Business Win* by Gene Kim, Kevin Behr, and George Spafford (2013: IT Revolution Press)

- *Theory of Constraints* by Eliyahu M. Goldratt (1990: North River Press)

- *The Unicorn Project: A Novel About Developers, Digital Disruption, and Thriving in the Age of Data* by Gene Kim (2019: IT Revolution Press)

- *Value Stream Mapping: How to Visualize Work and Align Leadership for Organizational Transformation* by Karen Martin and Mike Osterling (2014: McGraw-Hill Education)

Websites

Title	URL
Dev	https://dev.to/t/devops
DevOps Online	https://www.devopsonline.co.uk
DevOps.com	https://devops.com
The New Stack	https://thenewstack.io/category/devops
Reddit	https://www.reddit.com/r/devops
Tech Beacon	https://techbeacon.com/devops

Blogs

Title	URL
Agile Sysadmin	https://agilesysadmin.net
Agile Web Operations	https://agileweboperations.com
Atlassian Blog	https://www.atlassian.com/blog
AWS DevOps Blog	https://aws.amazon.com/blogs/devops
Azure DevOps Blog	https://devblogs.microsoft.com/devops
Barry O'Reilly	https://barryoreilly.com/blog
BMC Blogs: DevOps	https://www.bmc.com/blogs/categories/devops
Devco.net	https://www.devco.net
The DevOps Blog	https://thedevops.blog
DevOps Cube	https://devopscube.com/blog
DevOps Journal	http://devopsjournal.ulitzer.com
DevOps New Zealand	https://devops.nz
DevOpsGroup Blog	https://www.devopsgroup.com/blog
DevOpsNet	https://devopsnet.com
Flux7	https://blog.flux7.com
Fractional	https://fractio.nl
Google Cloud Blog	https://cloud.google.com/blog/products/gcp

IT Revolution	https://itrevolution.com/devops-blog
Just Enough Developed Infrastructure	http://www.jedi.be/blog
Kartar.net	https://www.kartar.net
ReleaseTEAM Blog	https://www.releaseteam.com/blog
Ryn Daniels	https://www.ryn.works/blog
SivaSai's DevOps Technical Blog	https://sivasaisagar.blogspot.com
XebiaLabs DevOps Blog	https://blog.xebialabs.com

Newsletters

Provider	URL
Appops Reloaded	https://tinyletter.com/mhausenblas
Better Dev Link	https://betterdev.link
DevOps Cube	https://devopscube.com
DevOps Dispatch	https://devopsdispatch.com
Devops Weekly	https://www.devopsweekly.com
DevOpsCon	https://devopscon.io/newsletter-en
DevOps'ish	https://devopsish.com
IBM Developer Newsletters	https://developer.ibm.com/newsletters/devops
Infrastructure as a Newsletter	https://www.digitalocean.com/community/newsletter
Last Week in AWS	https://www.lastweekinaws.com
Monitoring Weekly	https://monitoring.love
The New Stack	https://thenewstack.io/newsletter-archive
O'Reilly	https://www.oreilly.com/emails/newsletters
ReleaseTEAM	https://www.releaseteam.com/newsletter
Software Lead Weekly	http://softwareleadweekly.com
StatusCode Weekly	https://weekly.statuscode.com

Podcasts

Title	URL
All Things DevOps	https://allthingsdevops.bigbinary.com/archive.html
Arrested DevOps with Trevor Hess, Jessica Kerr, Bridget Kromhout, Joe Laha, and Matty Stratton	https://www.arresteddevops.com
Continuous Discussions	https://electric-cloud.com/c9d9-devops-podcast
DevOps Café with Damon Edwards and John Willis	http://devopscafe.org
DevOps Chats	https://devops.com/category/devops-chat/
DevOps Days Podcast	https://devopsdays.libsyn.com
DevOps and Docker with Bret Fisher	https://podcast.bretfisher.com/episodes
DevOps Interviews with Donovan Brown	https://channel9.msdn.com/blogs/devops-interviews
DevOps Paradox with Viktor Farcic and Darin Pope	https://www.devopsparadox.com
DevOps Radio	https://devopsradio.libsyn.com
Devops.fm with Brian Randell and Mickey Gousset	https://devops.fm
Durable DevOps with Gregory Bledsoe and Conor Delanbanque	https://soundcloud.com/user-542300749
Real World DevOps with Mike Julian	https://www.realworlddevops.com/episodes
ThoughtWorks	https://soundcloud.com/thoughtworks

Videos

Title	URL
"DevOps Tools"	https://www.youtube.com/watch?v=L0tnG23lVEc
"DevOps Tutorial for Beginners"	https://www.youtube.com/watch?v=ZtvpS5eVVDs
"How Netflix Thinks of DevOps"	https://www.youtube.com/watch?v=UTKIT6STSVM
"The DevOps Toolchain"	https://www.youtube.com/watch?v=bwE8aFPAzj8
"What Is DevOps? In Simple English"	https://www.youtube.com/watch?v=_I94-tJlovg

Online Courses

General

Provider	Courses
EDUREKA! https://www.edureka.co	• DevOps Certification Training
EDX https://www.edx.org	• DevOps for Developers: How to Get Started • DevOps Practices and Principles • Introduction to DevOps: Transforming and Improving Operations
LINKEDIN LEARNING https://www.linkedin.com/learning	• DevOps Foundations
UDACITY https://www.udacity.com	• Intro to DevOps
UDEMY https://www.udemy.com	• A Complete Guide to Modern DevOps Implementation • DevOps Boot Camp • DevOps Essentials • DevOps Fundamentals • DevOps Fundamentals: Gain Solid Understanding • DevOps: The Pre-Requisite Course • DevOps Tutorial: Complete Beginners Training— 5 in 1 Bundle • Get Into DevOps: The Masterclass • Learning Path: Modern DevOps • Mastering DevOps • Professional DevOps

Culture

Provider	Courses
COURSERA https://www.coursera.org	• DevOps Culture and Mindset
UDEMY https://www.udemy.com	• DevOps Culture • Implementing DevOps: Transforming Company Culture

Continuous Integration, Delivery, and Deployment

Provider	Courses
COURSERA https://www.coursera.org	• Continuous Delivery & DevOps • Continuous Integration
EDX https://www.edx.org	• Continuous Integration and Continuous Deployment
LINKEDIN LEARNING https://www.linkedin.com/ learning	• Continuous Integration: Tools • DevOps Foundations: Continuous Delivery/Continuous Integration
UDEMY https://www.udemy.com	• CI CD Pipeline: DevOps Automation in 1 Hr

Infrastructure as Code

Provider	Courses
LINKEDIN LEARNING https://www.linkedin.com/ learning	• DevOps Foundations: Infrastructure as Code
EDX https://www.edx.org	• Infrastructure as Code

Containers

Provider	Courses
LINKEDIN LEARNING https://www.linkedin.com/ learning	• DevOps Foundations: Containers

Security

Provider	Courses
LINKEDIN LEARNING https://www.linkedin.com/ learning	• DevOps Foundations: DevSecOps • DevSecOps: Automated Security Testing • DevSecOps: Building a Secure Continuous Delivery Pipeline • DevSecOps: Continuous Application Security
UDEMY https://www.udemy.com	• Practical DevOps Security

Testing

Provider	Courses
EDUREKA! https://www.edureka.co	• Continuous Testing in DevOps
EDX https://www.edx.org	• DevOps Testing

Monitoring and Feedback

Provider	Courses
EDX https://www.edx.org	• Application Monitoring and Feedback Loops
LINKEDIN LEARNING https://www.linkedin.com/ learning	• DevOps Foundations: Monitoring and Observability

NOTE

Most of the courses listed here do not focus on a specific tool or tools. Rather, they deal with more general DevOps concepts. There are, however, many tool-centric courses available online.

Webinars

Source & Title

DEVOPS.COM
https://devops.com/webinars

- 4 Steps: How to Value Stream Map Your Software Pipelines
- 10 Tips for Achieving Cultural Change in DevOps
- CI + CD + Release Orchestration: See Why It's Better Under One Roof
- CI/CD for Microservices Best Practices
- Continuous Delivery: The One Question You Must Answer
- Continuous Testing: A Critical Part of the DevOps Process
- DevOps for Database
- DevOps Quality Metrics That Matter: Forrester Research on 75 Common Metrics
- Embracing DevSecOps with Embedded Application Security
- Enterprise-Grade DevOps Solutions for a Start Up Budget
- Gary Gruver: Building Quality into the Software Development Process
- Igniting an Enterprise Technology Transformation with Ross Clanton & John Willis
- Inserting Security into DevOps Pipelines the Fast Way
- Migrating to Microservices: It's Easier Than You Think!
- Security in CI/CD Pipelines: Tips for DevOps Engineers
- Value Stream Management and the Next Decade of DevOps

RED HAT ANSIBLE
https://www.ansible.com/resources/webinars-training

- From Legacy to DevOps: Modernizing Application Infrastructure
- Optimize Automation: Model Everything, Deploy Continuously

WEBINARA
https://www.webinara.com

- Starting a DevOps & Continuous Delivery Transformation in the Enterprise
- Testing Infrastructure as Code with Security: 5 Practical Tips
- Turbocharge Your Continuous Delivery with Test Automation

TIP

DevOps.com is a great source for free, on-demand DevOps webinars.

DevOps Certification

Certificate	URL
Amazon Web (AWS)	https://aws.amazon.com/training
Atlassian	https://www.atlassian.com/university/certification
Chef	https://training.chef.io/certification
Docker	https://success.docker.com/certification
Google Cloud	https://cloud.google.com/certification
Jenkins	https://www.cloudbees.com/jenkins/jenkins-certification
Kubernetes	https://www.cncf.io/certification/ckad
Microsoft Azure	https://www.microsoft.com/en-us/learning/azure-exams.aspx
Puppet	https://puppet.com/learning-training/certification/?
Red Hat Ansible	https://www.ansible.com/products/training-certification
Splunk	https://www.splunk.com/en_us/training.html

DevOps Organizations

Organization	URL
Amazon Web Services (AWS)	https://aws.amazon.com
Atlassian	https://www.atlassian.com
Broadcom	https://www.broadcom.com
Chef	https://www.chef.io
CloudBees	https://www.cloudbees.com
CollabNet	https://www.collab.net
Compuware	https://www.compuware.com
Cucumber	https://cucumber.io
DevOps Institute	https://devopsinstitute.com
DevOps Research & Assessment (DORA)	https://cloud.google.com/devops
Docker	https://www.docker.com

(continues…)

DevOps Organizations (continued)

Organization	URL
Git	https://git-scm.com
GitHub	https://github.com
GitKraken	https://www.gitkraken.com
GitLab	https://about.gitlab.com
IBM (DevOps tools)	https://www.ibm.com/certify/index
Jenkins	https://jenkins.io
JetBrains	https://www.jetbrains.com
JFrog	https://jfrog.com
Microsoft (Azure)	https://azure.microsoft.com
Perforce	https://www.perforce.com
Puppet	https://puppet.com
Red Hat Ansible	https://www.ansible.com
ReleaseTEAM	https://www.releaseteam.com
SmartBear	https://smartbear.com
SonarSource	https://www.sonarsource.com
Sonatype	https://www.sonatype.com
Splunk	https://www.splunk.com
ThoughtWorks	https://www.thoughtworks.com
Travis CI	https://travis-ci.org
VMware	https://www.vmware.com
WANdisco	https://www.wandisco.com
XebiaLabs	https://xebialabs.com

Standards and Bodies of Knowledge

Organization & URL

Axelos
https://www.axelos.com/best-practice-solutions/itil

The Business Analysis Body of Knowledge (BABOK)
https://www.iiba.org/standards-and-resources/babok

Capability Maturity Model Integration (CMMI) Institute
https://cmmiinstitute.com

CD Foundation
https://cd.foundation

Cloud Native Computing Foundation
https://www.cncf.io

Institute of Electrical and Electronics Engineers (IEEE)
Computer Society Software Engineering Body of Knowledge (SWEBOK)
https://www.computer.org/education/bodies-of-knowledge/software-engineering

Institute of Electrical and Electronics Engineers Standards Association (IEEE-SA)
https://standards.ieee.org

International Electrotechnical Commission (IEC)
https://www.iec.ch

International Organization for Standardization (ISO)
https://www.iso.org/home.html

International Organization for Standardization (ISO)
9001 Quality Management System Standard
https://www.iso.org/iso-9001-quality-management.html

International Organization for Standardization (ISO)/
International Electrotechnical Commission (IEC) Joint Task Committee (JTC)
1 Special Committee (SC) 7: Software and Systems Engineering Standards
https://www.iso.org/committee/45086.html

The Linux Foundation
https://www.linuxfoundation.org

Project Management Institute Project Management Body of Knowledge (PMBOK)
https://www.pmi.org/pmbok-guide-standards

Conferences

Agile + DevOps	GitLab Commit
All Day DevOps	GitLab Contribute
AnsibleFest	GlueCon
Atlassian Summit	GoTo
AWS re:Inforce	IBM IoT Exchange
AWS re:Invent	IBM Think
ChefConf	Illuminate Sumo Logic User Conference
CloudBees Days	IoT Device Security Conference
DeliveryConf	JFrog swampUP
DevOps + Automation Summit	Lucidchart Connect
DevOps Enterprise Summit	Microsoft Ignite
DevOpsCon	Open Source Software Conference (OSCON)
DevOpsDays	Powershell + DevOps Global Summit
DevOpsWorld	Puppetize PDX
DevSecOps Days	QCon
DevSecCon	SmartBear Connect 2020
DockerCon	Splunk .conf
Git Merge	STAREAST
GitHub Universe	STARWEST

B APPENDIX

Tools for DevOps Success

This appendix categorizes tools that relate to nearly every aspect of DevOps. A brief description of each tool follows.

A few words on this appendix: First, this is not a complete list, although it is fairly thorough. Second, what tools are available may have changed by the time you read this book, as new tools regularly emerge (and others become obsolete). Third, this list includes tools from vendors regardless of whether I use them in my own work. In other words, it's vendor-agnostic.

NOTE

Some of the tools listed here have played a significant part in DevOps' expansion, including Kubernetes, Docker, Jenkins, and Spinnaker.

Planning Tools

Collaboration

These tools enable teams to share information, provide comments, eliminate ineffective handoff procedures, and track issues, no matter where team members are. The tools replace more traditional forms of communication, such as meetings and e-mail.

Atlassian Confluence	IBM Engineering Workflow Management
Atlassian Trello	Slack
CollabNet Version One	

Project Management

These tools are used to establish strategies, develop roadmaps, and decompose requirements into individual tasks, as well as to prioritize, assign, and schedule tasks, track time, and generate reports.

Atlassian Jira Align	Broadcom Rally Software
Atlassian Jira Core	IBM Rational DOORS
Atlassian Jira Software	Tempo

Requirements Management

These tools record new requests and break them into individual tasks.

Atlassian Jira Software	IBM Rational DOORS

Create Tools

Source Code Management (SCM) and Version Control

These tools store source code in a single repository. They also support automatic version control, change tracking, audit history, and documentation storage.

Apache Subversion	IBM Rational ClearCase
Atlassian Bitbucket	Perforce Helix 4Git
Git	Perforce Helix Core
GitHub	Perforce Helix TeamHub
GitLab	

SCM Clients

Using local SCM clients rather than cloud-based repositories enables team members to work on the same codebase from their own local machines.

Atlassian Sourcetree	Axosoft GitKraken

Database Automation

These tools allow unattended processes and self-updating procedures to perform administrative database tasks.

Datical	Delphix Dynamic Data Platform
DBmaestro	Redgate Flyway

Asset Management

These tools enable teams to reuse items during the development stage to ensure their code contains everything needed for each build.

JFrog Artifactory	Sonatype Nexus

Testing Tools

Testing

These tools enable you to capture code execution and user operations, use them to create a test case, and automate the entire test cycle from within the application.

Apache JMeter	Mocha
Cucumber	Perforce Helix QAC
Eggplant Performance and Load Testing	Perforce Helix Swarm
FitNesse	Perforce Perfecto
Gatling	Sauce Labs
IBM Engineering Test Management	Selenium
Jasmine	SmartBear SoapUI
JUnit	TestNG
Karma	Tricentis Tosca
Locust	Watir
Micro Focus Fortify Static Code Analyzer (SCA)	
Micro Focus Unified Functional Testing (UFT) One	

Code Review
These tools expedite the code review process to ensure fast feedback.

Atlassian Crucible   SmartBear Collaborator
Gerrit Code Review

Build Management and Automation Tools

Build Management and Automation
Developers use these tools to compile code changes before release. During the build process, scripts generate documentation, execute previously defined tests, compile the code, distribute related binaries, and more.

CloudBees Accelerator   IBM Rational ClearCase
GNU Make   IBM UrbanCode Build

Continuous Integration (CI)
These tools automate version control, track changes, trigger builds and tests, and may support automatic deployment.

AWS CodeBuild   Jenkins
Atlassian Bamboo   Jenkins X
CircleCI   JetBrains TeamCity
CloudBees CodeShip   Microsoft Azure DevOps Server
Compuware ISPW   OpenMake DeployHub
Google Tekton   ThoughtWorks Go
Hudson   Travis CI
IBM UrbanCode Build

Release Tools

Release Orchestration
These tools enable you to orchestrate releases across different tools, environments, and teams.

CloudBees Flow   Plutora Release Management
IBM UrbanCode Release   XebiaLabs XL Release
Jenkins

Continuous Delivery (CD) and Continuous Deployment (CD)

These tools constantly commit code and conduct automated QA and infosec tests. They can also automate the deployment process so that as soon as software passes all automated checks, it is pulled into production.

AWS CodeDeploy	IBM UrbanCode Deploy
AWS CodePipeline	Jenkins
Broadcom Automic Continuous Delivery Director	JetBrains TeamCity
CloudBees Accelerator	Octopus Deploy
CloudBees CodeShip	OpenMake DeployHub
CloudBees Core	Red Hat Ansible
CloudBees Flow	Spinnaker
Codefresh	ThoughtWorks Go
Compuware ISPW	XebiaLabs XL Deploy
GoCD	

Configuration Tools

Configuration Management

These tools automatically identify tasks, tools, documents, equipment, and components, and allow for the management of related revisions or versions.

Apache ZooKeeper	Red Hat Ansible
CFEngine	RUDDER
Chef	Rundeck
IBM Rational ClearCase	SaltStack Enterprise
Puppet	

Infrastructure as Code

These tools allow automatic resource provisioning.

Chef	HashiCorp Terraform
HashiCorp Packer	

Virtual Machines (VMs) and Containers

These tools are used to create applications.

Apache Mesos	Kubernetes
AWS Elastic Container Service (ECS)	Microsoft Azure Kubernetes Services (AKS)
Docker Enterprise	Rancher
Google Kubernetes Engine (GKE)	Red Hat OpenShift Container Platform
HashiCorp Vagrant	rkt
Helm	VMware

Cloud

These tools enable geographically separate teams to create, test, release, and monitor software without compromising code integrity, and they provide added automation capabilities.

Alibaba Cloud	IBM Cloud
Apache OpenWhisk	Microsoft Azure
AWS	OpenStack
CenturyLink Cloud Application Manager	Red Hat OpenShift Container Platform
Cloud Foundry	VMware vCloud Suite
Google Cloud	WANdisco

Ticketing and Monitoring Tools

Change Management

These tools provide formal approval workflows for new code and store each change's audit history.

Atlassian Jira Software	CollabNet Version One
BMC Helix ITSM	IBM Rational ClearQuest

Incident Management

These tools capture and report issues and categorize issues and route information about an issue to relevant teams.

Atlassian Jira Software	BMC Helix ITSM
Atlassian Opsgenie	PagerDuty
Atlassian Statuspage	

Issue Tracking

These tools find, record, and track bugs and defects.

Atlassian Jira Software	IBM Rational ClearQuest

Analytics

These tools deliver actionable information such as test pass rates, build stability, bug tracking, and defect logging. They also provide insight into areas such as performance, task processing, release cycles and frequencies, and development process compliance.

AppDynamics	Nagios XI
Atlassian Fisheye	New Relic One
CloudBees DevOptics	ServiceNow
Datadog	Splunk
Dynatrace	XebiaLabs XL Impact
Elastic Elasticsearch	Zabbix
Elastic Kibana	Zenoss
JFrog Mission Control	

Security Tools

Security

These tools scan for, detect, and alert developers about suspicious code snippets in product code.

Checkmarx Static Application Security Testing (CxSAST)
JFrog Xray
Signal Sciences Runtime Application Self Protection (RASP)
Sonatype Nexus
Synopsys Black Duck
Veracode Greenlight

IT Service Management Tools

IT Service Management (ITSM)

These tools ensure regulatory compliance and system security.

Atlassian Jira Service Desk	ServiceNow

Tool Suites and Centralized Tool Management

Tool Suites

Each of these suites contains a series of tools that work together to complete each step of the development cycle.

Atlassian	JFrog Enterprise+ Platform
AWS	Microsoft Azure DevOps Server
CollabNet	Perforce HelixALM Suite
GitLab	XebiaLabs

Centralized Tool Management

For organizations that choose not to use a streamlined tool suite, a centralized tool management tool can help ensure the various tools used work well together.

ConnectALL	Tasktop

Tool Descriptions

Alibaba Cloud
https://us.alibabacloud.com
Provides cloud computing services to online businesses. **CATEGORY:** Cloud

Amazon Web Services (AWS)
https://aws.amazon.com
A group of cloud computing tools that delivers a comprehensive platform for the software development and delivery processes. AWS offers more than 90 services, including tools for storage, computing, networking, deployment, traditional development, and mobile development.
CATEGORY: Continuous Integration (CI), Cloud, Tool Suites

Apache JMeter
https://jmeter.apache.org
Open source software that tests functional behavior and measures performance.
CATEGORY: Testing

Apache Mesos
http://mesos.apache.org
Open source software that manages computer clusters. **CATEGORY:** VMs and Containers

Apache OpenWhisk
https://openwhisk.apache.org
An open source serverless cloud platform. It uses Docker containers to manage infrastructure, servers, and scaling. **CATEGORY:** Cloud

Apache Subversion
https://subversion.apache.org
An open source software versioning and version control system.
CATEGORY: SCM and Version Control

Apache ZooKeeper
http://zookeeper.apache.org
A centralized service that maintains configuration information and performs other tasks that help develop distributed applications.
CATEGORY: Configuration Management

AppDynamics
https://www.appdynamics.com
Monitors applications in real time to detect anomalies and yield business insights.
CATEGORY: Analytics

Atlassian Bamboo
https://www.atlassian.com/software/bamboo
Unites the CD pipeline with a single workflow, automating builds, tests, and deployments to enable you to release code more frequently. A server-hosted solution that supports all types of languages and integrates several other technologies, Bamboo provides complete control over the CD and CI processes.
CATEGORY: Continuous Integration (CI)

Atlassian Bitbucket
https://bitbucket.org
A centralized repository management tool for proprietary code. Available in the cloud, within a datacenter, or on your company's own servers, Bitbucket enables teams to collaborate on code and to streamline build, test, and release processes, improving the CD pipeline. CATEGORY: SCM and Version Control

Atlassian Confluence
https://www.atlassian.com/software/confluence
Enables teams to collaborate and share knowledge from a central location. It works best when used in conjunction with Atlassian Jira Software. CATEGORY: Collaboration

Atlassian Crucible
https://www.atlassian.com/software/crucible
Provides lightweight, workflow-driven tools to facilitate collaborative code reviews.
CATEGORY: Code Review

Atlassian Fisheye
https://www.atlassian.com/software/fisheye
Enables you to track, search, and visualize changes to your codebase. You can also integrate Fisheye with Crucible to track code-review activities and receive change notifications as they occur. CATEGORY: Analytics

Atlassian Jira Align
https://www.atlassian.com/software/jira/align
Makes work visible to align everyone across the organization and improve productivity.
CATEGORY: Project Management

Atlassian Jira Core
https://www.atlassian.com/software/jira/core
Provides a centralized view of tasks to surface insights into projects and initiatives.
CATEGORY: Project Management

Atlassian Jira Service Desk
https://www.atlassian.com/software/jira/service-desk
Quickly detects incidents and issues so you can deal with them as they arise. For best results, integrate Jira Service Desk with Jira Software and Confluence. CATEGORY: ITSM

Atlassian Jira Software
https://www.atlassian.com/software/jira
Can be used to quickly plan, track, and release code. CATEGORY: Project Management, Requirements Management, Incident Management, Issue Tracking, ITSM

Atlassian Opsgenie
https://www.atlassian.com/software/opsgenie
An incident management system that integrates with monitoring, ticketing, and collaboration tools to centralize alerts and route incidents to the right resources.
CATEGORY: Incident Management

Atlassian Sourcetree
https://www.sourcetreeapp.com
A free Git user interface for use on Windows and Macintosh machines. Sourcetree enables you to improve how you manage your code by using detailed branching diagrams. CATEGORY: SCM Client

Atlassian Statuspage
https://www.statuspage.io
Provides real-time status information regarding your system or components to users and customers. CATEGORY: Incident Management

Atlassian Trello
https://www.atlassian.com/software/trello
An Agile project management tool. With Trello, you can build detailed project boards to track every aspect of a project. CATEGORY: Collaboration

AWS CodeBuild
https://aws.amazon.com/codebuild
A cloud-based tool that provisions build servers, compiles source code, runs test, and produces ready-to-deploy software packages. CATEGORY: Continuous Integration (CI)

AWS CodeDeploy
https://aws.amazon.com/codedeploy
Automates the deployment process.
CATEGORY: Continuous Delivery (CD) and Continuous Deployment (CD)

AWS CodePipeline
https://aws.amazon.com/codepipeline
Automates the build, test, and deployment processes after each code change.
CATEGORY: Continuous Delivery (CD) and Continuous Deployment (CD)

AWS Elastic Container Service (ECS)
https://aws.amazon.com/ecs
Allows you to easily run and scale containerized applications.
CATEGORY: VMs and Containers

Axosoft GitKraken
https://www.gitkraken.com
A free Git GUI client for Windows. GitKraken also offers Kanban board capabilities.
CATEGORY: SCM Client

BMC Helix ITSM
https://www.bmc.com/it-solutions/bmc-helix-itsm.html
Offers intelligent, predictive ITSM tools across a multi-cloud environment.
CATEGORY: Change Management, Incident Management

Broadcom Automic Continuous Delivery Director
https://www.broadcom.com/products/software/automation/continuous-delivery/
automic-continuous-delivery-director
Builds development pipelines in minutes and tracks the progress of new features and
releases across development.
CATEGORY: Continuous Delivery (CD) and Continuous Deployment (CD)

Broadcom Rally Software
https://www.broadcom.com/products/software/agile-development/rally-software
Aligns daily work with strategy and enables you to leverage data to steer business
decisions. CATEGORY: Project Management

CenturyLink Cloud Application Manager
https://www.ctl.io/cloud-application-manager
Orchestrates and automates the delivery of infrastructure, applications, and services
on various public cloud services. CATEGORY: Cloud

CFEngine
https://cfengine.com
Enables users to automate and manage their IT infrastructure.
CATEGORY: Configuration Management

Checkmarx Static Application Security Testing (CxSAST)
https://www.checkmarx.com/products/static-application-security-testing
Scans source code early in the software development cycle to identify vulnerabilities
and provide insights for remediating them. CxSAST currently supports over 20 coding
and scripting languages. CATEGORY: Security

Chef
https://www.chef.io
Converts infrastructure into code to automate the provisioning of development,
testing, and deployment environments.
CATEGORY: Configuration Management, Infrastructure as Code

CircleCI
https://circleci.com
Automates the development pipeline from commit to deploy.
Category: Continuous Integration (CI)

Cloud Foundry
https://www.cloudfoundry.org
An open source tool that makes it faster and easier to build, test, deploy, and scale applications using any of several cloud providers and developer frameworks.
Category: Cloud

CloudBees Accelerator
https://www.cloudbees.com/cloudbees-accelerator
Speeds up build times and shortens QA and infosec testing cycles to carve out more time for experimentation and iteration. **Category:** Build Management and Automation, Continuous Delivery (CD) and Continuous Deployment (CD)

CloudBees CodeShip
https://www.cloudbees.com/products/cloudbees-codeship
Provides a simple CI environment that supports everything from microservices to monoliths and can integrate with all major cloud service providers.
Category: Continuous Integration (CI), Continuous Delivery (CD) and Continuous Deployment (CD)

CloudBees Core
https://www.cloudbees.com/products/cloudbees-core
An end-to-end automation engine for CI and CD.
Category: Continuous Delivery (CD) and Continuous Deployment (CD)

CloudBees DevOptics
https://www.cloudbees.com/products/cloudbees-devoptics
Identifies bottlenecks and optimizes the value stream. **Category:** Analytics

CloudBees Flow
https://www.cloudbees.com/products/cloudbees-flow
Enables you to predictably deploy any application to any environment at any scale, and to manage release pipelines across teams, tools, and environments.
Category: Release Orchestration, Continuous Delivery (CD) and Continuous Deployment (CD)

Codefresh
https://codefresh.io
Enables you to use containers to quickly build, integrate, and deploy code. Containers are reusable across pipelines.
Category: Continuous Delivery (CD) and Continuous Deployment (CD)

CollabNet
http://www.collab.net
A single secure platform for collaboratively developing software applications.
Category: Tool Suites

CollabNet Version One
https://www.collab.net/products/versionone
Unifies teams and enables them to envision and deliver great software.
CATEGORY: Collaboration

Compuware ISPW
https://www.compuware.com/ispw-source-code-management
Shows the status of all programs and code throughout the life cycle, automates deployments, and performs other tasks related to CI, CD, and continuous deployment.
CATEGORY: Continuous Integration (CI), Continuous Delivery (CD) and Continuous Deployment (CD)

ConnectALL
https://www.connectall.com
Integrates software delivery tools from different vendors into a more seamless system.
CATEGORY: Centralized Tool Management

Cucumber
https://xebialabs.com/technology/cucumber
A free, open source, platform-agnostic automated testing tool. CATEGORY: Testing

Datadog
https://www.datadoghq.com
Aggregates metrics and events throughout the pipeline. CATEGORY: Analytics

Datical
https://www.datical.com
Automatically deploys database changes to eliminate bottlenecks.
CATEGORY: Database Automation

DBmaestro
https://www.dbmaestro.com
Automates and governs database releases to minimize downtime and data loss.
CATEGORY: Database Automation

Delphix Dynamic Data Platform
https://www.delphix.com/platform
Provisions lightweight, compressed copies of production data in minutes while keeping everything in sync. CATEGORY: Database Automation

Docker Enterprise
https://www.docker.com/products/docker-enterprise
A platform-as-a-service (PaaS) that facilitates the use of containers in the development process. CATEGORY: VMs and Containers

Dynatrace
https://www.dynatrace.com/platform
An application performance management product that offers end-to-end visibility of the development pipeline. CATEGORY: Analytics

Eggplant Performance and Load Testing
https://www.eggplantsoftware.com/performance-and-load-testing
A simple load-testing tool with analysis and reporting capabilities. CATEGORY: Testing

Elastic Elasticsearch
https://www.elastic.co/products/elasticsearch
A fast search and analytics engine. CATEGORY: Analytics

Elastic Kibana
https://www.elastic.co/products/kibana
Works with Elastic Elasticsearch to visually represent your data. CATEGORY: Analytics

FitNesse
http://fitnesse.org
A wiki web server that works as an open source acceptance testing tool.
CATEGORY: Testing

Gatling
https://gatling.io
An open source load-testing tool that can be integrated into the development pipeline. CATEGORY: Testing

Gerrit Code Review
https://www.gerritcodereview.com
Enables teams to quickly and easily review code in an integrated way.
CATEGORY: Code Review

Git
https://git-scm.com
A free, open source, command-line version control system that enables users to track changes in source code. CATEGORY: SCM and Version Control

GitHub
https://github.com
A GUI-based platform to leverage Git. It also includes additional features, including tools for task management and collaboration. CATEGORY: SCM and Version Control

GitLab
https://about.gitlab.com
A complete end-to-end Git-based DevOps platform that operates as a single application. CATEGORY: SCM and Version Control, Tool Suites

GNU Make
https://www.gnu.org/software/make
Controls the generation of executable files and other non-source files of a program from the program's source files. CATEGORY: Build Management and Automation

GoCD
https://www.gocd.org
A free open source CI/CD server that enables users to easily visualize and model complex workflows. CATEGORY: Continuous Delivery (CD) and Continuous Deployment (CD)

Google Cloud
https://cloud.google.com
Provides a world-class cloud infrastructure and a robust set of tools (software development and otherwise). CATEGORY: Cloud

Google Kubernetes Engine (GKE)
https://cloud.google.com/kubernetes-engine
Provides a production-ready environment for deploying containerized applications.
CATEGORY: VMs and Containers

Google Tekton
https://cloud.google.com/tekton
A Kubernetes-native open source framework for creating CI and CD systems.
CATEGORY: Continuous Integration (CI)

HashiCorp Packer
https://www.packer.io
A lightweight, fast, and flexible open source tool for creating identical machine images for multiple platforms from a single source configuration.
CATEGORY: Infrastructure as Code

HashiCorp Terraform
https://www.terraform.io
Enables users to define infrastructure as code to manage the full software development cycle. CATEGORY: Infrastructure as Code

HashiCorp Vagrant
https://www.vagrantup.com
A tool for building and managing VM environments in a single workflow to reduce development environment setup time and increase production parity.
CATEGORY: VMs and Containers

Helm
https://helm.sh
A package manager for Kubernetes. CATEGORY: VMs and Containers

Hudson
http://hudson-ci.org
A free CI tool for use with several version control applications.
CATEGORY: Continuous Integration (CI)

IBM Cloud
https://www.ibm.com/cloud
A robust set of tools for use on the cloud, including tools for DevOps.
CATEGORY: Cloud

IBM Engineering Test Management
https://www.ibm.com/us-en/marketplace/test-management
Enables teams to collaborate, plan, build, and execute tests. CATEGORY: Testing

IBM Engineering Workflow Management
https://www.ibm.com/us-en/marketplace/workflow-management
Facilitates collaboration and teamwork to better plan, manage, track, and share work.
CATEGORY: Collaboration

IBM Rational ClearCase
https://www.ibm.com/us-en/marketplace/rational-clearcase
A scalable version control and SCM tool that makes all development-related assets accessible from a single source. CATEGORY: SCM and Version Control, Build Management and Automation, Configuration Management

IBM Rational ClearQuest
https://www.ibm.com/us-en/marketplace/rational-clearquest
A change management and issue tracking tool that works with numerous processes, tools, and development workflows. CATEGORY: Change Management, Issue Tracking

IBM Rational DOORS
https://www.ibm.com/us-en/marketplace/requirements-management-doors-next
A centralized, scalable, adaptable project management and requirements management tool that helps capture, trace, analyze, and manage information changes.
CATEGORY: Project Management, Requirements Management

IBM UrbanCode Build
https://developer.ibm.com/urbancode/products/urbancode-build
Facilitates the scaling, configuration, and management of the build infrastructure and its integration with development, testing, and release tooling.
CATEGORY: Build Management and Automation, Continuous Integration (CI)

IBM UrbanCode Deploy
https://developer.ibm.com/urbancode/products/urbancode-deploy
Automates application deployments throughout environments.
CATEGORY: Continuous Delivery (CD) and Continuous Deployment (CD)

IBM UrbanCode Release
https://developer.ibm.com/urbancode/products/urbancode-release
A collaborative release-management tool. CATEGORY: Release Orchestration

Jasmine
https://jasmine.github.io
A behavior-driven development framework with a clean and obvious syntax for testing JavaScript code. CATEGORY: Testing

Jenkins
https://jenkins.io
A free open source automation server that enables both CI and CD. Jenkins provides hundreds of plug-ins to help automate the development process as well as build and deploy software. CATEGORY: Continuous Integration (CI), Release Orchestration, Continuous Delivery (CD) and Continuous Deployment (CD)

Jenkins X
https://jenkins-x.io
Provides pipeline automation and other tools to help teams collaborate.
CATEGORY: Continuous Integration (CI)

JetBrains TeamCity
https://www.jetbrains.com/teamcity
A build management and CI server that supports CI out of the box.
CATEGORY: Continuous Integration (CI), Continuous Delivery (CD) and Continuous
Deployment (CD)

JFrog Artifactory
https://jfrog.com/artifactory
A repository manager that enables users to handle every code update from a single
repository and to manage build, test, and release workflows.
CATEGORY: Asset Management

JFrog Enterprise+ Platform
https://jfrog.com/enterprise-plus-platform
Offers an end-to-end pipeline to facilitate CD, CI, and continuous deployment.
CATEGORY: Tool Suites

JFrog Mission Control
https://jfrog.com/mission-control
A configurable dashboard that offers a high-level view of the entire delivery pipeline.
CATEGORY: Analytics

JFrog Xray
https://jfrog.com/xray
Identifies security and flaws in artifacts stored in a repository.   CATEGORY: Security

JUnit
https://junit.org/junit4
A simple framework for writing repeatable tests. CATEGORY: Testing

Karma
http://karma-runner.github.io
A testing environment that offers instant feedback. CATEGORY: Testing

Kubernetes
https://kubernetes.io
An open source system for automatically scaling, managing, and deploying
containerized applications. CATEGORY: VMs and Containers

Locust
https://locust.io
An open source load-testing tool. CATEGORY: Testing

Micro Focus Fortify Static Code Analyzer (SCA)
https://www.microfocus.com/en-us/products/static-code-analysis-sast/overview
Integrates with other tools to build security testing into the development process.
CATEGORY: Testing

Micro Focus Unified Functional Testing (UFT) One
https://www.microfocus.com/en-us/products/unified-functional-automated-testing/overview
Offers end-to-end testing. **CATEGORY:** Testing

Microsoft Azure
https://azure.microsoft.com
A cloud platform that offers application development tools, among others.
CATEGORY: Cloud

Microsoft Azure DevOps Server
https://azure.microsoft.com/en-us/services/devops/server
A collaborative software development platform. **CATEGORY:** Tool Suites

Microsoft Azure Kubernetes Service (AKS)
https://azure.microsoft.com/en-us/services/kubernetes-service
Facilitates the deployment and management of containerized applications through serverless Kubernetes, an integrated CI and CD experience, and enterprise-grade security and governance. **CATEGORY:** VMs and Containers

Mocha
https://mochajs.org
A JavaScript test framework that performs asynchronous testing. It is hosted on GitLab.
CATEGORY: Testing

Nagios XI
https://www.nagios.com/products/nagios-xi
Offers comprehensive application, service, and network monitoring in one centralized solution. **CATEGORY:** Analytics

New Relic One
https://newrelic.com/platform
Combines telemetry data in one place so you can visualize everything that's happening across your software environment, as well as find and fix problems.
CATEGORY: Analytics

Octopus Deploy
https://octopus.com
Enables you to manage releases and to automate complex application deployments and operations tasks.
CATEGORY: Continuous Delivery (CD) and Continuous Deployment (CD)

OpenMake DeployHub
https://www.deployhub.com
A central microservices sharing platform where developers catalog, publish, version, and deploy microservices and other reusable components. **CATEGORY:** Continuous Integration (CI), Continuous Delivery (CD) and Continuous Deployment (CD)

OpenStack
https://www.openstack.org/software
A cloud operating system that controls large pools of compute, storage, and networking resources. **CATEGORY:** Cloud

PagerDuty
https://www.pagerduty.com
Analyzes data to identify incidents and notifies and empowers people to take action.
CATEGORY: Incident Management

Perforce Helix 4Git
https://www.perforce.com/products/helix4git
A Helix Core server and a Git connector to perform Git commands for version
control purposes. CATEGORY: SCM and Version Control

Perforce Helix Core
https://www.perforce.com/products/helix-core
A version control system that securely versions all content in a single repository.
CATEGORY: SCM and Version Control

Perforce Helix QAC
https://www.perforce.com/products/helix-qac
A C and C++ code analyzer. CATEGORY: Testing

Perforce Helix Swarm
https://www.perforce.com/products/helix-swarm
A free web-based code-review tool for use with Helix Core. CATEGORY: Testing

Perforce Helix TeamHub
https://www.perforce.com/products/helix4git
A GUI-based platform to leverage Git. It's available on-premises or on the cloud.
CATEGORY: SCM and Version Control

Perforce HelixALM Suite
https://www.perforce.com/products/helix-alm
A modular suite of tools for each step required during the application lifecycle
management process. CATEGORY: Tool Suites

Perforce Perfecto
https://www.perfecto.io
A cloud-based continuous testing platform. CATEGORY: Testing

Plutora Release Management
https://www.plutora.com/platform/release-management
Enables you to define and schedule releases, track dependencies, manage approvals,
and maintain compliance while accelerating change. CATEGORY: Release Orchestration

Puppet
https://puppet.com
An open source tool that automates the provisioning of infrastructure.
CATEGORY: Configuration Management

Rancher
https://rancher.com
Deploys and manages Kubernetes clusters. It includes tools for running Kubernetes
in the enterprise for both development and operations groups.
CATEGORY: VMs and Containers

Red Hat Ansible
https://www.redhat.com/en/technologies/management/ansible
A universal language solution to automate infrastructure, applications, networks, security and compliance tasks, as well as cloud and container deployments. It provides a user-friendly interface with centralized control and configuration of system integrations. CATEGORY: Continuous Delivery (CD) and Continuous Deployment (CD), Configuration Management

Red Hat OpenShift Container Platform
https://www.openshift.com/products/container-platform
Offers a hybrid cloud foundation for building and scaling containerized applications. CATEGORY: VMs and Containers, Cloud

Redgate Flyway
https://flywaydb.org
Acts like version control for your database, simplifying database migration. CATEGORY: Database Automation

rkt
https://coreos.com/rkt
A container engine for cloud-native environments. CATEGORY: VMs and Containers

RUDDER
https://www.rudder.io
A platform for automating and maintaining production infrastructure. CATEGORY: Configuration Management

Rundeck
https://www.rundeck.com
Schedules jobs and automates routine processes across development and production environments. CATEGORY: Configuration Management

SaltStack Enterprise
https://www.saltstack.com/products/saltstack-enterprise
Quickly provisions, deploys, and configures any infrastructure, including physical and virtual servers, public and private clouds, containers, and more. CATEGORY: Configuration Management

Sauce Labs
https://saucelabs.com/solutions/automated-testing
An automated testing solution that integrates seamlessly with popular CI and CD tools. CATEGORY: Testing

Selenium
https://www.seleniumhq.org
Automates web applications for testing purposes and other tasks. CATEGORY: Testing

ServiceNow
https://www.servicenow.com/now-platform.html
Digitizes workflow to ensure work moves smoothly across silos and departments. CATEGORY: Build Management and Automation, Analytics, ITSM

Signal Sciences Runtime Application Self Protection (RASP)
https://www.signalsciences.com/products
Secures applications with context-aware protection to allow development teams to continuously deploy. **Category:** Security

Slack
https://slack.com
A communications hub that enables you to organize conversations, share files and documents, find old messages and files, and more. **Category:** Collaboration

SmartBear Collaborator
https://smartbear.com/product/collaborator
Offers comprehensive code-review capabilities, supports real-time updates, and integrates with several SCMs. **Category:** Code Review

SmartBear SoapUI
https://www.soapui.org
An API test automation framework. **Category:** Testing

Sonatype Nexus
https://www.sonatype.com/product-nexus-repository
Offers a single source of truth for all artifacts, components, and binaries in a system. **Category:** Asset Management, Security

Spinnaker
https://www.spinnaker.io
An open source, multi-cloud CD platform that enables you to release software changes quickly. **Category:** Continuous Delivery (CD) and Continuous Deployment (CD)

Splunk
https://www.splunk.com
Captures, indexes, and correlates data into a searchable repository to yield important business and process insights. **Category:** Analytics

Synopsys Black Duck
https://www.blackducksoftware.com
Enables you to keep track of open source code in your product to mitigate security and license compliance risks. **Category:** Security

Tasktop
https://www.tasktop.com
Integrates tools used in the development cycle to offer a complete view of all tools used at every point in the CI and CD pipeline. **Category:** Centralized Tool Management

Tempo
https://www.tempo.io
Works with Atlassian products to help teams collaborate, plan, and schedule resources. **Category:** Project Management

TestNG
https://testng.org/doc
A framework for writing repeatable tests. It was inspired by JUnit but has additional functionality. **CATEGORY:** Testing

ThoughtWorks Go
https://www.thoughtworks.com
Enables you to visualize and streamline your value stream to facilitate CI and continuous deployment. **CATEGORY:** Continuous Integration (CI), Continuous Delivery (CD) and Continuous Deployment (CD)

Travis CI
https://travis-ci.com
A CI service that integrates with GitHub to help build and test software applications. **CATEGORY:** Continuous Integration (CI)

Tricentis Tosca
https://www.tricentis.com/products
A continuous testing platform that allows testing early in the development cycle. **CATEGORY:** Testing

Veracode Greenlight
https://www.veracode.com/products/greenlight
Scans code as it's being written for security flaws to offer immediate feedback to developers. **CATEGORY:** Security

VMware vCloud Suite
https://www.vmware.com/products/vcloud-suite.html
VMware vCloud Suite is a private cloud solution. **CATEGORY:** VMs and Containers, Cloud

WANdisco
https://www.wandisco.com
A cloud provider that provides advanced replication services to improve system availability for data storage and code repositories. **CATEGORY:** Cloud

Watir
http://watir.com
An open source Ruby library for automating tests. **CATEGORY:** Testing

XebiaLabs
https://xebialabs.com
An end-to-end DevOps-oriented development platform. **CATEGORY:** Tool Suite

XebiaLabs XL Deploy
https://xebialabs.com/technology/xl-deploy
An automatic deployment tool that lets you deploy, roll back, and diagnose issues without writing or maintaining scripts or workflows. **CATEGORY:** Continuous Delivery (CD) and Continuous Deployment (CD)

XebiaLabs XL Impact
https://xebialabs.com/technology/xl-impact
Contains integrated KPIs to track the health of your CD pipeline, reveal trends, predict outcomes, and recommend actions. CATEGORY: Analytics

XebiaLabs XL Release
https://xebialabs.com/technology/xl-release
A release management tool specifically for CD. CATEGORY: Release Orchestration

Zabbix
https://www.zabbix.com
An all-in-one monitoring solution. CATEGORY: Analytics

Zenoss
https://www.zenoss.com/solutions/devops
Includes tools to increase the deployment pipeline's end-to-end visibility.
CATEGORY: Analytics

Glossary

A

AGILE A lightweight approach to software development that combined aspects of Toyota Production System (TPS), total quality management (TQM), incremental development, iterative development, and Lean.

ANDON CORD A cord found in manufacturing plants that use Toyota Production System (TPS). Anytime a worker experiences a problem during production, they pull this cord to shut down the line and swarm the problem. Some software companies follow this same practice (though without the physical cord).

AUTOMATION Using a mechanical or electronic device to complete a process or task instead of using human labor.

AUTOMATION ENGINEER Someone who identifies tasks that can be automated and who designs, implements, and monitors automation processes to handle those tasks.

B

BETA TESTING A test that involves sending a product or feature under development to a select group of users.

BLAMELESS POST-MORTEM A meeting that occurs after any failure to hash over what happened without issuing blame.

BOTTLENECK Any point in a system that clogs the flow. Another word for bottleneck is *constraint*.

BUREAUCRATIC ORGANIZATIONAL CULTURE A rules-oriented organizational culture. Organizations with a bureaucratic culture tend to be highly siloed and allow minimal collaboration.

BURNOUT A stress-induced physical or mental breakdown.

C

CHANGE MANAGEMENT The process of identifying and implementing required changes within a computer system in a controlled manner.

CLOUD A network of remote servers for storing, managing, and processing data.

CLOUD COMPUTING Using resources on the cloud, rather than a local server or personal computer, to store, manage, and process data.

CLOUD ENGINEER Someone who designs, plans, manages, maintains, and supports technology associated with the cloud—for example, virtual machines used to provision programming environments or host applications.

CODE REVIEW A form of feedback that involves one engineer examining the work of another either immediately before or immediately after the code is committed.

COMMAND AND CONTROL A top-down management style in which management issues orders on what to do and how to do it.

CONSTRAINT *See* bottleneck.

CONTAINER A standard unit of software that packages an application's code and all its dependencies together. The result is an application that runs quickly and reliably from one computing environment to another.

CONTINUOUS DELIVERY (CD) A software-engineering approach that allows shorter development cycles and in which code is constantly kept in a deployable state.

CONTINUOUS DEPLOYMENT (CD) A software-engineering approach that allows for shorter development cycles and in which code is constantly deployed to an operations or operations-like environment.

CONTINUOUS IMPROVEMENT An ongoing cycle of improvement in the quality of processes, services, and products. These might be sweeping improvements or incremental ones.

CONTINUOUS INTEGRATION (CI) The practice of continually committing small batches of code and using automated testing to validate changes.

D

DATABASE ADMINISTRATOR Someone who works closely with systems administrators and operations engineers to ensure that all databases used throughout the company, including for software development, are up to date and working correctly.

DEPLOY To deliver the code for a feature, set of features, or product to a production environment.

DEPLOYMENT PIPELINE The DevOps workflow, which is a manifestation of an organization's value-stream map.

DevSecOps A term highlighting the practice of shifting security tasks left in the development cycle.

DOGFOODING A type of beta test in which company employees test a product or feature themselves to identify bugs, glitches, and other problems.

E

EMPLOYEE ENGAGEMENT The degree to which employees are committed to doing their jobs to the fullest of their ability, and to which the company is committed to ensuring employees reach their full potential.

ENTERPRISE ARCHITECT Someone who bridges the gap between the business function and the IT function. Essentially, the enterprise architect translates the product or feature put forth by the product manager for IT and develops a concrete plan for its production.

EXTRINSIC MOTIVATION When someone is moved to do something by some external reward, such as money or praise, or fear of punishment for not doing. Opposite of intrinsic motivation.

F

FIREFIGHTING Dealing with the emergencies that inevitably arise due to high levels of technical debt.

FIRST WAY One prong in a three-pronged approach to DevOps articulated by Gene Kim. The First Way is "systems thinking."

FULL-STACK ENGINEER Someone who has a basic grasp of every step in the software development process and all associated technologies.

G

GATE Anything that results in a wait condition—setup time, queue time, or wait time.

GENERATIVE ORGANIZATIONAL CULTURE An organizational culture that de-emphasizes hierarchy and promotes collaboration and trust for improved performance.

H

HANDOFF Turning over work from one team to another.

HIERARCHICAL An organizational structure that looks like a pyramid, with the CEO at the top.

I

INCREMENTAL DEVELOPMENT A waterfall system in which work is broken into small pieces, or batch sizes. As each small piece completes a phase, the system progresses to the next one.

INFRASTRUCTURE AS A SERVICE (IaaS) A resource delivery model in which third-party providers host servers, storage, and other compute resources for use by customers.

INTRINSIC MOTIVATION When someone is driven to do something for its own sake, because it's interesting or satisfying in and of itself. Opposite of extrinsic motivation.

ITERATIVE DEVELOPMENT A system in which work is broken into small pieces, and in which the linear waterfall system is bent into a circle. With iterative development, code is designed, developed, and tested in repeated or iterative cycles until it is ready to deploy.

J–L

JUST-IN-TIME (JIT) PRODUCTION A production system that seeks to make only what is needed, only when it is needed, and only as much as needed.

KANBAN BOARD A tool that makes work processes visible, with columns for each stage of the value stream and cards for each task. When work on an item is complete, its card is moved to the next column to show its progress.

LEAN A variation on Toyota Production System (TPS) that seeks to abolish any process or product that does not add value for the customer. Lean also seeks to smooth and optimize workflow by paying special attention to bottlenecks.

M

MICROSERVICES ARCHITECTURE A software architecture that breaks the product into several tiny single-purpose components called services. *See also* service.

MINIMUM VIABLE PRODUCT (MVP) The simplest version of a product or feature that still delivers its core functionality.

MISSION CONTROL A management style in which leaders supply employees with a vision but leave them to complete that mission however they see fit.

MONOLITHIC ARCHITECTURE A software architecture in which a product is composed of a single code base (or perhaps a few layers of code).

O

OPERATIONS ENGINEER Someone who ensures that all end user–facing systems are up and running.

OPPORTUNITY COSTS The costs incurred by not investing in developing a product or feature that people want to use.

ORGANIZATIONAL CULTURE The unspoken priorities, beliefs, conflicts, and power dynamics within a company.

P

PATHOLOGICAL ORGANIZATIONAL CULTURE An organizational culture that is power-oriented. In organizations with a pathological culture, higher-ups use threats and fear to motivate employees.

Π (PI) FORMATION A team structure in which the team has deep knowledge in two functional areas with more limited proficiency in others, or are stocked with individuals who are experts in two fields.

PLATFORM AS A SERVICE (PAAS) A software delivery model in which customers access and use platforms and tools to develop, deploy, and manage software products.

PROCESS TIME The time a resource (person or machine) spends actually working on a piece of work.

PRODUCT MANAGER Someone who identifies a need for a product or feature and ushers it from its inception to its release and beyond.

Q

QUALITY ASSURANCE (QA) ENGINEER Someone who ensures that code meets all quality and regulatory standards.

QUEUE TIME The time a piece of work spends waiting for a resource (person or machine) to finish something else before starting on it.

R

RELEASE To make a feature, set of features, or product available to some or all of your customers.

RELEASE ENGINEER Someone who ensures that all hardware and software components in a product or feature work together as they should.

RETROSPECTIVE A meeting in which the team discusses what was successful about the development cycle, what could have been improved, and how to repeat the successes and incorporate the improvements in the future.

S

SCOPE CREEP Describes when the goals of a project expand while the project is in progress. Scope creep often causes projects to take longer than they should.

SCRUM A daily team meeting in which team members update each other on what they did yesterday, what they plan to do today and, if applicable, any obstacles.

SECOND WAY One prong in a three-pronged approach to DevOps articulated by Gene Kim. The Second Way is "amplify feedback loops."

SECURITY ENGINEER Someone who ensures that code is secure—free of bugs, holes, and other vulnerabilities.

SERVICE 1. A modular piece of code that handles a specific application function. 2. A resource accessed from the cloud, such as Software as a Service (SaaS), Platform as a Service (PaaS), and Infrastructure as a Service (IaaS).

SETUP TIME The time a piece of work spends waiting for a resource (person or machine) to be set up to complete it.

SHIFTING LEFT The practice of performing tasks associated with downstream groups earlier in the development cycle.

SILO A team or group that works in isolation from others.

SITE RELIABILITY ENGINEER (SRE) Someone who incorporates aspects of software engineering to infrastructure and operations problems. The main goals of the SRE are to create scalable and highly reliable software systems.

SOFTWARE AS A SERVICE (SAAS) A software delivery model in which customers access and use software online instead of installing it on their own computers.

SOFTWARE CONFIGURATION MANAGEMENT Processes to manage, organize, and control changes in code and other items during product development.

SOFTWARE DEVELOPER Someone who writes the source code that serves as the foundation of a digital product, service, or feature.

SUBJECT MATTER EXPERT (SME) Someone who has great expertise in a technical topic.

SYSTEMS ADMINISTRATOR Someone who is responsible for the smooth operation of the computer and network systems used in the course of daily business (including for software development).

T

T FORMATION A team structure in which the team has deep knowledge in one functional area with limited proficiency in others.

TECHNICAL DEBT The long-term price of short-term decisions like taking shortcuts or putting off planned or preventive work.

THEORY OF CONSTRAINTS A managerial philosophy that dictates that organizations focus on the bottleneck (constraint) at the expense of all other improvements until that bottleneck is eliminated and a new bottleneck is identified.

THIRD WAY One prong in a three-pronged approach to DevOps articulated by Gene Kim. The Third Way is "culture of continual experimentation and learning."

THREE WAYS A three-pronged approach to DevOps articulated by Gene Kim. The Three Ways are "systems thinking," "amplify feedback loops," and "culture of continual experimentation and learning."

TOTAL QUALITY MANAGEMENT (TQM) A variation on Toyota Production System (TPS) that optimizes the waterfall approach to improve quality but does not give much consideration to the human side of things.

TOYOTA PRODUCTION SYSTEM (TPS) A work system developed by Toyota Motor Corporation that optimizes the waterfall approach. TPS is particularly concerned with continual improvement, the human aspects of work, and eliminating waste.

TRANSFORMATIONAL LEADERSHIP A leadership style characterized by vision, intellectual stimulation, inspirational communication, supportive leadership, and personal recognition.

V

VALUE STREAM The detailed sequence of steps that occur during the design, development, and distribution of a product or feature.

VALUE-STREAM MAP A document that lists every step in the value stream.

VANITY METRIC A metric on which you cannot act.

VENDOR LOCK-IN When a company has invested so much in tools from one vendor that switching to another, better vendor becomes cost prohibitive.

VERSION CONTROL Creating a new version of a product or feature under development each time a developer commits code, generating a unique name or number to identify it and saving information in the form of metadata about the commit (such as who initiated it and when).

VIRTUAL MACHINE (VM) A software program that emulates a computer, complete with its own operating system and applications. When a VM is installed on a computer, users can access it by using the host computer in person or by connecting to it via network or the cloud.

W

WAIT CONDITION Something that creates a delay in the production process. Wait conditions include setup time, queue time, and wait time.

WAIT TIME The time a piece of work spends waiting for some other piece of work to be completed, so the two pieces of work can be assembled together.

WASTE 1. The transportation of products, people, or tools. 2. Excessive inventory or excessive motion by machines or people. 3. Waiting, overproduction, overprocessing, or defects.

WATERFALL A process-intensive work model that breaks development activities into a series of phases that are completed one at a time and sequentially.

Index

A

A/B testing (customer feedback), 69–70
accountability (positive learning culture), 81
adapting, 120
administrators
    database administrators, 96
    systems administrators, 95–96
Agile
    DevOps relationship, 16
    Manifesto for Agile Software Development, 13
    overview, 12–13
    waterfall model comparison, 3
allocating resources, 118–120
amplifying feedback loops. *See* fast feedback
analytics tools, 145
Andon Cord, 80
architects (enterprise architects), 95
asset management tools, 141
attitudes (career development), 111–113
automatic environment provisioning, 46–47
automating
    automation engineers, 99–100
    build automation
        continuous integration, 43–44
        tools, 142
    configuration management
        engineers, 100
        tools, 143
    databases, 141
    job security, 100
    tasks (continuous delivery), 49–50
    test automation engineers, 98–99
    testing
        continuous integration, 45–46
        fast feedback, 59–61
automation engineers, 99–100
autonomy (cross-functional teams), 29–30

B

behaviors (career development), 111–113
beta testing (customer feedback), 67–68
blame (positive learning culture)
    blameless post-mortems, 79
    zero blame, 80–81
blameless post-mortems, 79
blogs, 128–129
bodies of knowledge, 137
body language, 106–107
books, 127
bottlenecks
    defined, 4
    value stream, 35, 37–40
bug tracking tools, 145
build automation
    continuous integration, 43–44
    tools, 142
burnout
    positive learning culture, 86–88
    teams, 7
businesses. *See* organizations

C

career development. *See also* resources; roles
    attitudes, 111–113
    behaviors, 111–113
    overview, 103
    personal qualities, 111–113
    skills/knowledge
        bodies of knowledge, 137
        body language, 106–107
        collaboration skills, 108–110
        communication skills, 105–108
        conflict, 109–110
        nonverbal communication, 106–107
        overview, 104–105
        proxemics, 107
    training/education
        certification (DevOps), 111, 135
        overview, 110–111

www.ingramcontent.com/pod-product-compliance
Lightning Source LLC
Chambersburg PA
CBHW071151050326
40689CB00011B/2066